How to Write a Resume That Will Score

Interviews and Land the Job

And Much More

101 World Class Expert

Facts, Hints, Tips and Advice

on Resumes

Information is power – you know that. But, how do you research the best Resume writing strategies, without spending too much of your time (and money) on it? The average person earns $ 1100 per week, which equates to $ 27 per hour. Trying to do the research yourself would take you at least 5 hours to come up with the best information, AND you'll have to do this on a regular basis to come up with the most up to date and current information.

There has to be a different way to find the info you want! Well, yes there is... we did all the research for you, combed through all the information and got down to the hard core of the 101 most up to date and best Facts, Hints, Tips and Advice here, in this book.

The 101 of the most current, most actual and beneficial Facts, Hints, Tips and Advice you can find from experts in the field on Resume writing:

2 'New' Cover Letters to Get You Hired!

5 Insider Tips You Must Know For Writing Your Executive Resume

A Quick Guide on Cover Letter Format

A Resume Format

Acupuncturist CV - How to Write Them Effectively

Administrative Cover Letters

An Insider's Guide to Scan-Proofing Your Online Resume

Attorney Resume - Blue-Chip Pass For Potential Clients

Biggest Failure of Job Applicants - Not Mentioning Their Accomplishments

Blank Resume Form Free of Charge

Cover Letter Are Not Cover Letters - They Are Sales Letters

Cover Letter Examples - Available on the Internet

Cover Letter For Resume - What You Need to Know

Cover Letter Templates Work

Cover Letter Writing in a Jiffy

Cover Letters

Cover Letters - A Few Sample Tips

Cover Letters - More Than Just a Dust Cover For Your Resume

Cover Letters - When Applying For a Job

Crafting the Perfect CV - Perils, Pitfalls and Pratfalls

Creating a Resume - How Do You Go About It?

Creating Your First Resume

Darn Good Reasons Why You Should Or Should Not Hire A Professional Resume Service

Need Help With Resume?

Professional Cover Letter Format

Resume 101 - Proofreading Your Resume - Sink Or Swim?

Resume Advice - Optimizing Your Resume For Federal Government Jobs

Resume Assistance For You

Resume Cover Letters - What Do You Need to Include?

Resume Do's and Don'ts For 2009

Resume Format Sample - Tips, Tips, and More Tips

Resume Formats - Chronological Or Functional, Which One Best Suits You?

Resume Length - The Truth Hurts

Resume Maker Software - Get a Competitive Advantage Using Resume Maker Software

Resume Miseries - Are You Making Any of These 3 Deadly Mistakes With Your Resume?

Resume Style Tips For the Worker Who Can't Get Hired

Resume Tips For Financial Candidates

Resume Writing - 5 Words You Should Never Use on Your Resume

Resume Writing - Are You a Less Than Perfect Candidate?

Resume Writing Blues - They're Just Not That Into You!

Resume Writing Services May Be Your Only Chance of Getting Noticed

Resume Writing Tips - 4 Vital Things to Remember When Writing a Resume

Resumes - 3 Secrets For How to Start Writing a Resume That Will Score Interviews and Land the Job

Resumes - Powerful Secrets For Managers to Score Interviews and Land the Job You Really Want

Simple Resume Tip

The 7 Secrets to Resume Writing and Business Success

The Basics Behind the Right Cover Letter Format

The Problems With Resume Writing

The Resume Service

Tips For Maximizing the Effectiveness of Your Resume

Top 3 Tips How to Format a Winning CV

Top 7 Resume Writing Tips

Waitress Resume - Writing the Resume That Gets That Job

Ways to Write a Resume

What a Cover Letter Can Do That a Resume Can't Do

What Every Executive Should Know About Writing a Powerful Resume

What Job Resume Format Should You Use?

Table of Contents

What Every Executive Should Know About Writing a Powerful Resume

With all the discussion surrounding today's job market, one key fact seems to be lost: there's never been so many choices available to employers.

Many hiring authorities are literally under siege, and the speed of Internet-powered executive searches only adds to the situation.

What this means for executives is that a marketing focus is critical, and that, more than ever, converting your resume into a marketing brochure is an essential step.

To get into the marketing mindset and sharpen your promotional skills, start envisioning your resume as a marketing brochure, using these key attributes:

1) Technical writing.

Resumes are intended to provide analytical and precise detail about your background and achievements.

In fact, resume writing has a strong correlation to technical writing in that both professions demand extreme precision.

Most readers of your resume will assume that what you show on paper correlates strongly to what you can do for your next employer.

If your resume fails to show results (meaning key metrics and bottom-line, quantifiable information), the hiring audience will dismiss your resume since it lacks PROOF of your perform-ance.

For this reason, it's important to recognize the significance of what you've done at work. To get at the level of detail that will actually market your qualifications, use a blank piece of paper to create 2 columns on a single page.

In the first column, list all the major tasks and projects you've been involved with at work.

In the corresponding row, list the result that each project had on the company.

This can be efficiencies gained during a business process improvement effort, costs cut with the implementation of a new system, or new business gained by creating customer relation-ships.

Think in terms of dollars saved, numbers of people affected, or amount of business generated, and you'll be on the right track.

Remember that the more analytical and precise these re-sults are, the better. Whatever the result, it should first be noted on your list, then incorporated into your resume.

2) Business knowledge and subject matter expertise.

As many job hunters know, resumes are often scanned by automated systems for keyword information in order to reject or accept the document for a job opening. However, did you realize that the same keyword information also has an effect on the HUMAN reader?

Since hiring authorities are frequently on the lookout for core business competencies, including keywords on your resume gives you a means of showing proficiency in your field.

The best way to mine for this information is to study your own business and industry expertise, and pull in some key phrases that describe your knowledge.

In addition, these keywords can be gleaned from systems, methodologies, leadership styles, and other components of your everyday work.

You can also comb through job descriptions for your desired position to obtain more keywords for use on your resume.

After you've identified these skills, be sure to weave this information throughout your resume, keeping in mind that employers need to see HOW you've applied these competencies.

3) A true leadership presentation.

Style and formatting are often-overlooked components in the success of a resume, yet a striking and compelling presentation can win over the reader--and make your skills more marketable.

As an example, try opening Microsoft Word and selecting the basic resume template for review.

Then, as a comparison, look on the Internet for "executive resume samples" to see some core differences. You should see understated, elegant presentations that make the information seem more interesting to read, and bring out various words more than others.

Don't discount the impact of this strategy, since it is often used to re-weight certain parts of your background-and position you squarely into a new role.

To add emphasis to your resume presentation, consider using format elements, such as italics, borders, bold text, and lines. This will help to set off certain phrases or skills.

In addition, continue to use the resume samples you've found to incorporate a new design element here and there.

Think of it as borrowing key ideas that can help you promote your skills.

In summary, thinking like a marketing and technical copywriter can be an effective strategy for creating your resume.

After all, it's important to design a true marketing campaign that promotes your strengths--and gets employers to look deeper into the value you offer--in order to claim the attention your career deserves.

Laura Smith-Proulx <http://www.anexpertresume.com/about.htm> , Certified Career Management Coach, Certified Professional Resume Writer, and Certified Interview Coach, is a former recruiter and the Executive Director of An Expert Resume <http://www.anexpertresume.com> , a career services firm that caters to organizational leaders. Published in 6 career bestsellers and cited for global resume industry awards, she wins interviews for executives at all levels with compelling and powerful leadership presentations.

How to Kill the Perfect Cover Letter

It is amazing that with all of the advice available on writing a great cover letter, mistakes continue to be made. This isn't to say hat you have to be perfect 100% of the time, but you do need to trive for perfection.

So how to you kill a great cover letter?

- Grammar and Spelling: Not only is this the fastest way to uin a cover letter, it is also the most preventable. Proofreading our cover letter will ensure that you won't be rejected for pre- entable mistakes. It only take a few minutes and it can make all ne difference in landing an interview.

- Informal Language: Your cover letter is a formal piece of orrespondence and not the place for informal language. Avoid lang and conversational language and ensure that the tone of our letter stays professional.

- Generic Text: Another major mistake made by job hunt- rs. For many people, the job hunt is a numbers game. It is easy to last out resumes to every job posting that you come across, with a eneric cover letter attached. However, if you don't give the re- ruiter the sense that you are interested in their company, success ill be hard to come by. Tailor your cover letter to the specific ompany and you will have more "luck".

- Lying: This is self explanatory. If you are caught lying, you on't even make it to the interview. Even worse, if your lie is aught after you are hired, it is grounds for immediate dismissal.

- Unsigned Letter: A simple mistake but one that is easy to nake. If you forget to sign your cover letter, it will give the wrong npression to the interviewer. Double check that each letter you end our has your signature.

- Missing Contact Information: If you don't let them know ow to contact you, how do you expect to land an interview?

- No Objective: Your cover letter is the start of your per- onal sales pitch. If the employer doesn't know what you are elling, or even what job you are applying to, then it is easy to iscount you as an applicant. Make sure that you state up front who you are, what you have to offer, and what job you are applying to.

- Too Long: You don't want to overwhelm the reader at first sight. Keep your cover letter brief. It should be no more than one page and should contain no more than five paragraphs.

Keep these pitfalls in mind and you are on your way to a perfect cover letter.

Trevor Wilson is a recent graduate and the founder of Gradversity.com <http://www.gradversity.com> . The site, launched in 2008, is dedicated to helping new graduates find their first real job. You can find his daily posts, resources, and other great job-hunting advice at http://www.gradversity.com.

Resumes - 3 Secrets For How to Start Writing a Resume That Will Score Interviews and Land the Job

Starting a resume is a daunting task for almost everyone. What should I include? How do I describe what I did? What is most important?

This can be a real problem if you already found a position that looks like a perfect match for your qualifications. You may start to doubt yourself, and any enthusiasm you had for the job can be lost quickly.

The best place to start, when writing your resume, is with the facts about your employment history. Keep in mind that simple and positive is a whole lot better than complicated and confusing.

Start with these steps and you'll be well on your way to Landing The Job You Really Want:

1. MAKE A LIST OF EACH COMPANY THAT YOU'VE WORKED FOR

Start by listing the company name, location (city and state are fine), and the start and end dates. Use a separate sheet of paper for each company; you'll need the space for the questions that follow.

2. DESCRIBE THE COMPANY OR TEAM

If the company is well known, describe the team you worked for.

"Worked in Accounting supporting the Information Technology Department"

If the company is not well known, describe the product or service the company provides to its customers. How many people work at the company? How many customers does/did it have? Describe the customers: for example: Individuals, Other Companies, Government, Students

"Real Estate Technology Inc. has 57 employees and provides website design and programming services for large commercial real estate brokerage firms"

3. WHAT DID YOUR JOB ENTAIL?

Your next boss is going to be most interested in the WHAT, HOW, and WHO of your job responsibilities. WHAT were your responsibilities? HOW did it you do it? (What systems did you use? What skills were required?) WHO did you interact with (boss, customers, peers, other departments, subordinates, etc.)?

"Created and maintained a new computer system to calculate real-time profits. The system was developed in C++. Worked with senior management to gather key requirements and with the accounting group to validate calculations."

Ready to learn more about how to get more interviews <http://www.magneticresume.com> for each resume you send out?

Download my FREE 12-page report, "Anatomy of a Perfect Resume," at http://www.magneticresume.com so you can learn:

 *   The 4 most common deadly mistakes that people make and how to fix them!
 *   How to create the perfect Career Objective & Career Summary sections
 *   How to maximize your resume so you're the candidate your next boss wants to meet!

Scott Shane Holt has seen it all while hiring over 100 people on Wall Street, in good times and bad, and as an executive coach helping managers and other professionals accelerate their careers.

How to Write a Resume If You Have Time Gaps in Your Work History

Reasons a "Functional" Resume' may be a better choice than a "Chronological" Resume

As past owner of a reume writing service here in Greensburg, PA, I learned that for some clients, the functional resume' works better than the standard "chronological" resume'

Of the two main types of résumé's, chronological and functional, the chronological is the norm.. The functional resume' is usually written under the following circumstances:

You have time gaps in your work history. Could be for any number of reasons, but since busy screeners are looking for ways to reduce the pile of applicant résumé's down to a few, don't let them throw away your chance to interview.

If you've spent 10 years in the state penitentiary, a functional resume' may not help you but if you had a catastrophic injury, or lost your job and spent 3 months looking for another (not too uncommon these dayso a functional resume' might be your best bet.

Other good reasons are:

* You are older and have had so many jobs your chronological resume' is "too long."

* A change to a completely different career (little or no actual experience in your new field).

* You are a sharp go-getter with lots of achievements, but just graduated (no experience).

* Your job history is so extensive that it makes you look overqualified.

Although some employers don't like them, I think they have an advantage because they make your resume' stand out because the appearance is different.

To write a functional resume' you need to make a "highlights" summary. This list should show outstanding achievements, honor and awards, money saving suggestions you made, etc. You could include employer or educational institution names but omit the time frame.

Below this list you could type in the employer names, but omit the dates.

Whatever your reason for using a functional resume', be sure you are prepared to answer any questions you might get during a job interview about why you chose this format. Hope this brief article will help you get that interview and the job offer that may follow.

Frank Ernhart is a retired chemical engineer with a secondary career as a resume' writer and job getting consultant. Frank run a local resume service in Greensburg, PA for 3 years and has done hundreds of resume's for people from laborer to plant manager, etc. A self published book called "How to Get a Job Anywhere Anytime" available from Lulu.com is featured along with other topics on the website at http://www.frankernhart.com.

An Insider's Guide to Scan-Proofing Your Online Resume

Almost every online job application puts your computer through the scanner before it ever reaches human hands - sad, but true. If your resume isn't organized, or can't be properly read by the computer scanner, your resume might get tossed aside without even being touched by an actual human. If you're a fine match to the job, this is not only a loss to you, but a loss to the company you're applying to. However, you're the one fighting for a job in this economy, so you're the one who needs to make sure your resume gets through the initials traps and red tape. Here's how to change up your resume to make it through the technological trappings of the modern human resources world:

- Use descriptive nouns. Scanners recognize nouns more than verbs. So focus your resume with descriptive nouns that hone in on the job being offered, and how you fit into the description. The more nouns you use, the better your chance that you will hit some or all of the key words that scanner's set up to look for. As a general rule in resume writing, you want to use shorter, more commonly used words. This is essential for resumes read by computer scanners. Their vocabulary may be limited so you don't want to get too technical or full of jargon.

- Use your section keywords. Include your skill-set, education, experience, talents, abilities, and history. Computer scanners actively look for these sections so your potential employer can see that your resume is broken appropriately.

- Keep it simple. Scanners don't like designs or fancy graphics or fonts. If it can't read your resume, your resume may just get thrown out, instead. Use a standard font and basic format when submitting a resume online. Computers can understand white space between sections, so if you want to break your resume up to keep the formatting clean, this is a good way to space it out.

- Don't add graphs or charts. Even if you normally include graphs or charts in your resume, these are not appropriate when a computer is going to scan them, because, again, they can't read pictures and may cause a malfunction. You will have to convert these sections into text that is as interesting a read as your chart.

- Don't use abbreviations. Computers don't understand them - you have to spell everything out, including degrees.

- Use the standard name and address format. The top line should contain your first and last name, then the next lines your contact information.

- Length doesn't matter. Resumes meant for computer scanners can actually be up to to four pages in length, and your potential employer won't be put off. They'll be aware that you formatted your resume to help the scanner do its job - just don't stretch the information to impress them - make sure everything on the resume has the most impact possible.

It may seem that technology has made the the application process for sending your resume and getting an interview harder than ever, but once you know the in's and out's of what's expected, you'll stand apart from the crowd and have a leading edge on the competition. Very few people know how to format their resumes specifically for a computer scanner, so now, you're ahead of the game in many respects. Take the time to be prepared and take advantage of the opportunity to put your best foot forward by creating a resume that will not only get through the electronic obstacles, but into the hands of the person that will give you the interview.

Melissa Brewer is a freelance writer and author of The Little White Ebook of Virtual Assistant Jobs, the complete guide to administrative work available online, available at LittleWhiteE-book.com. She has been a small business owner for ten years and currently lives in Washington, DC, about 3 miles from the Obama White House.

Acupuncturist CV - How to Write Them Effectively

Most employers usually do not scan CVs/resumes for more than 30 seconds. As a result you should ensure that your acupuncturist CV follows the conventions which employers expect. Although rare, an employer may require a printed CV in which case you should use a laser printer with quality conqueror paper. Never send out photocopied resumes.

For acupuncturists, there is no hard and fast rule about the length of a CV but typically two pages should be enough to compile a good CV detailing your career, experience and qualifications as an acupuncturist. However, the CV of an acupuncturist with 25 years experience will have more information than someone recently qualified with 2 years experience; and it would not be unreasonable to expect a CV highlighting a 25 year career to extend beyond 2 pages.

The format of your CV should be simple and without clutter and the font style along with the font size should be consistent throughout the CV. The most widely adopted font styles are Times Roman and Arial. Font size 14 is adequate for headings and 10 is fine for the body of the document.

Your resume should begin with a professional profile in which you briefly state your background, career and intentions within the acupuncture profession, all within a single short paragraph consisting of a maximum of 4 sentences. Below the profile, you should highlight a bulleted list of your key skills. Theses skills are what make you an acupuncturist and employers will be looking for typical competencies here. Your list of skills should typically include mention of:

* A thorough understanding of complementary therapies
* Sound interpersonal skills and ability to listen, relate and communicate with patients
* Ability for putting together detailed history of patients
* Experience in undertaking thorough diagnosis of patients' conditions
* Experience in formulating sound course of treatment for patients
* Expertise in administering needles depending on the degree of sensitization needed
* Sound ability to create and maintain good customer/client relations
* Good business and management skills (for running a practice)

If you have recently qualified with little or no work experience as an acupuncturist, then the next section below your key skills should highlight your qualifications along with professional training. This should be followed by a brief description of your work experience. However, if you already have professional experience as an acupuncturist, then your professional work experience should precede your education/qualifications. In either case, always write in the third person and minimise use of "I" in your narrative. In highlighting your education and training, always mention dates, name of institutions attended and qualifications attained. Likewise, highlight your professional work experience with starting and leaving dates, name of employer, job title and brief description of what you did / achieve. Make liberal use of verbs in describing your remits and mention how you acquired, used and developed relevant skills and competencies.

Resource box: Richard Blake is a CV writer offering CV service <http://www.professional-cv-writingservices.co.uk> for school leavers, graduates, and professionals up to senior exectives and CEOs. Services also include professional cover letters

<http://www.professional-cv-writingservices.co.uk/professional-cover-letters.html> .

Cover Letter For Resume - What You Need to Know

When sending your resume to a potential employer, the most important part could be the cover letter for resume. This is your best change to get their attention. It could be your cover letter resume that determines whether or not you get the interview. Most of the time, this is when you make your initial impression and it is the cover letter that is used to find the best applicants. This is the time in which you can shine. You need to make the employer want to know more about you.

Your cover letter should outline why you want to be employed there, what you wish to acquire from the organization, and how you can contribute to the organization. You need to tell the employer why you would be the best pick for them. Remember, however, that your cover letter resume needs to be a supplement of your resume and not a duplicate of it. Tell the employer that you are excited to bring your skills to them and how they would benefit by hiring you. If you do not interest them, they will not interview you and, if they do not interview you, you can't get the job.

It is important to make it clear in your cover letter whether or not you are looking for just contacts or if you are looking for an immediate position.

When creating your cover letter resume, don't use the same template for all resumes. You need to create a different cover letter and a different resume for each of the companies you are applying to. They need to have a personalized touch. It is important that you realize you are telling that employer that you want to work for them and that you can be valuable to their company, so you don't want to send out the same cover letter to everyone.

And be sure that your resume cover letter does not contain a lot of useless information. You must get to the point by giving just enough information to make the employer want more of you, so don't write about your entire life. Be detailed in what part of yourself you are trying to sell to the employer. It has to remain professional because you need the employer to know that you are concerned with the type of impression you are relaying to them as a potential representative of their company.

Just make sure that your grammar is correct, as is your spelling. There is nothing more irritating than trying to give the impression that you are an educated professional and then presenting a cover letter and resume that looks to have been written by a child. This is not the impression you want to give a potential employer.

Cynthia Penfold reveals secrets on cover letter for resume <http://www.howtomakearesumeblog.com/cover-letter-for-resume/cover-letter-for-resume/> at her How To Make A Resume Blog <http://www.howtomakearesumeblog.com/> .

Cover Letters - More Than Just a Dust Cover For Your Resume

In today's demanding job environment, you need all the help you can get to stand out from the competition. The cover letter is your answer. Most all of your competition will use a standard boring cover letter or the same cover letter template they found in a resume book. This is where 90% of your competition will fall to the wayside as employers and hiring managers will simply toss the cover letter and resume aside.

But, by submitting an outstanding cover letter that "sells" you to the hiring manager or employer, you have a much better chance in securing that all important job interview. That's the key to a well crafted and professionally written letter. It sells you to the hiring manager or employer.

A well written cover letter should focus on how your skills, experience and personality, will benefit the company for the specific position you are applying for. You should not generalize your skills and experience. Make the letter like a focused laser beam aimed at the position you are applying for.

Basically, a resume tells what you have done in the past and your experience. A cover letter tells and employer how that experience can benefit the company. Think of the cover letter as your personal salesperson. Out there "selling" the benefits of your skills and experience, totally focused on the available open position. This is what will open the eyes of a hiring manager or employer.

Also remember, don't tell the employer what your hoping to get from the company or personal benefits your hoping to achieve with employment from the company. The employer wants to know, what can you do for me and why should I hire you over someone else.

Have the cover letter address the needs of the employer and you stand a much better chance in getting that all important job interview. Simply address the needs of the person reading your letter with a slant towards "selling you" for that targeted position.

For more information on how to write a killer Cover Letter, visit us at http://jobhuntingresources.info as well as other tips and information on finding that next great job.

Resumes - Powerful Secrets For Managers to Score Interviews and Land the Job You Really Want

If you are a manager and you're looking for a job, you are not alone.

In fact, I was at a dinner party last weekend, and as the conversation turned towards the economy, there was genuine surprise at the number of friends -- who are really good at what they do and who held senior positions -- who have been let go.

Managers face an additional set of challenges when looking for a job, because employers are interviewing you for two different skill-sets. You need to be able to lead and manage a team of people AND you need to have some degree of competency, expertise and domain knowledge within the team's job function.

Most managerial applicants stress their leadership skills at the expense of their domain expertise. They go wrong by describing themselves as generic managers.

You'll score more high level interviews when you balance leadership with domain expertise:

1. PORTRAY YOURSELF AS HANDS-ON

In fact, I recommend that you use the words "Hands-On Manager" to describe yourself. Employers want to know that you are actively involved in the day-to-day operations, understand the issues, and can take corrective action quickly.

2. STRESS YOUR PERSONAL CONTRIBUTIONS

Most managers underestimate the value of their involvement in a project. If you attend the kick-off meetings or brainstorming sessions, mention that on your resume. Your involvement and negotiations at the beginning of the projects, even though it might be for a short time, eliminate a lot of problems later on.

3. HOW YOU SUPPORT YOUR TEAM WHEN PROJECTS GO AWRY

When things go wrong, how do you handle it? Are you supportive of the team and push for what they need to get the job done? Do you push your folks for the best they can produce? Do you give credit, where credit is due? Think back over your career. When did you help a junior team member overcome an obstacle? It's really attractive to employers when you combine your expertise with your leadership skills, in order to produce outstanding results.

Ready to learn more about how to get more interviews <http://www.magneticresume.com> for each resume you send out?

Download my FREE 12-page report, "Anatomy of a Perfect Resume," at http://www.magneticresume.com so you can learn:

* The 4 most common deadly mistakes that people make and how to fix them!
* How to create the perfect Career Objective & Career Summary sections
* How to maximize your resume so you're the candidate your next boss wants to meet!

Scott Shane Holt has seen it all while hiring over 100 people, in good times and bad, and as an executive coach helping managers and other professionals accelerate their careers.

Graphic Designer's Resume - 5 Tips For Preparing Your Portfolio

A cover letter is an invitation to read your resume. You resume highlight your experience and to demonstrate your qualities as the right person for the job. But your portfolio is the most important aspect of your job hunt. Its sole purpose is to catch the hiring manager's attention and get you the interview or job. With so much depending on your portfolio, one may be tempted to do many of the very things hiring personnel frown upon in a portfolio.

This list is made for every designer that wants to create a portfolio. It's also useful for those designers who already have a portfolio but want to re-work on it.

1. Showcase your skills It's always a good idea to put various skills and styles you work on in your portfolio. This demonstrates your future employer that you are fluent in many styles an that he or she is getting a their money's when hiring you.

2. 10 to 12 examples Al though this may seem a pretty small number, it really isn't. You must choose which pieces are you strongest and that display you qualities as a creative professional. Too many pieces will bore the person viewing. Also keep in mind that you must choose jobs that really show what you can do, not jobs that mean a lot to you. Not because a job is your particularly favorite means it should be in your portfolio, so very critical about you work.

3. Show actual pieces If your work is in a magazine or newspaper, find some copies and tear out (cut actually) the page. Don't think that because you portfolio is on line that you do not have to do this. Always keep these sheets with you just in case. If you don't have any, for any reason, try to create a nice mock-up.

4. Have someone review it Not your mom or friend that has no idea what you are trying to do. Have a designer take a look at it and see if you are on the right track. If you by chance know a person who works in a human resources office or an art director, better yet. The key is to have people with a critical eye to review it.

5. Keep it up to date Even though it may seem a bit tedious, you should have your portfolio as updated as possible. You always want to show your most recent accomplishment. I suggest that before you remove and old job to replace it with a new one, have someone look to see if the change is the best one.

I can not stress enough how important your portfolio is. Give it the time and effort it deserves. Your portfolio might dictate your employment, so be very detailed oriented when creating it. Use these tips on you portfolio and good luck on you job hunting.

Juan C. Rivera

Web / Graphic Designer http://www.juan-key.com

From Logos to web pages, and more. Visit my website at the above link for more Graphic Design Services

Graphic Design Blog http://www.graphic-iti.com

Why a CV Sample May Be the Undoing in Your Job Quest - What You Should Know

The Human Resource departments of many leading firms are now getting past the days when it was the trend of job seekers to submit original resumes through post. In simple terms, the self-prepared resume is getting obsolete. This type of resume is fast being replaced by the online CV format. It is this type of CV that recruiters are now forwarding to prospective employers. Granted that many are still captivated by the free CV templates that are all over the Internet, it is only fair that we go through a couple of tips that will offer guidance in creating online resumes.

In the recent past, job seekers were encouraged to seek out the most attractive resume samples and then use these as templates to input their personal data. The aim was to come up with a CV that would deliver the personal information with the same npact as the CV sample did. It has been realized that these CV amples were incapable of producing the desired results.

The usage of templates and CV samples is gradually being 1ade redundant by virtue of the fact that the recruitment agencies ɔ which these CVs are sent are responsible for processing the ontained information. With this in mind it is suddenly dawning n people that all the effort of creating an eye-catching resume is 1ore or less wasted time.

What happens in the information processing procedure is uite straightforward. The recruitment agencies simply seek out 1e most vital details of the resume, extract these, reformat them, nd place them in a database. It is from this database that pro-pective employers make their searches. The basis of hire then ecomes the raw and helpful information that you provided. All 1e design layouts and formatting are put to naught. What then ould be the most informed decision for a job seeker going for-vard?

The creation of the online CV should be preceded by a tringent compilation of the most decisive information that the mployer will directly consider; it's all about your training, experi-nce, and skills.

- The dates of your schooling and job experience.
- The names of the firms you have worked for.
- What titles you held in these jobs and the responsibilities 1at were attached.
- What you achieved and accomplished at each of the jobs.
- What relevant skills you acquired that may be transferred ɔ the job in question.
- The professional associations you are a member to.
- Any works that you have published.
- Possible security clearances obtained.

Cynthia Penfold reveals secrets for a cv sample http://www.cv-sample.org/> at her How To Make A Resume log <http://www.howtomakearesumeblog.com/> .

How to Make a Resume - Tips

There are several ways that you can approach and learn more about making a winning resume. As long as you're using effective approaches, then you are guaranteed to make a resume that stands out and gets the attention of your prospective employer. There are actually two main components that need to be combined to create an impressive result. First, you have to know how to organize your content and format it. Second, you need to provide information that is accurate in regards to skills, education, experience, and your objective. When you are able to communicate these points effectively, you just might land the job interview.

In past years, graduates were in the habit of getting their advice about resumes from the placement offices within their universities. But with the advancement of technology, this is something that is not necessary because the Internet has got it all there ready for you to access. All you have to do is choose what you think is the most informative to get yourself started. There are websites that offer free templates and advice on how to make resumes. There are other websites that take it a little further by providing actual CV samples that you can look through to get a clear picture. Some sites may even ask you for payment so that they can do your resume for you.

It is not necessary for you to go for those services that cost you money when you can make a winning resume on your own. You only need to remember that making a resume consists of some basic rules. Your resume is your sole communication with a potential employer, making communication as clear as possible so that they can make an informed decision about you.

Whatever you decide to do, make sure your resume is free of error. There should be no typos or grammatical mistakes. You can make sure of this by proofreading several times and also requesting someone else to go through it. When you make your resume, refrain from recording any falsified information. There is nothing more humiliating than losing your job later because you were dishonest.

The resume should also not be a mess of words. Let the reader have a good time going through your resume. Try not to squeeze everything into one page, but use two or three if you need to.As you create your resume, let it be relevant to the job that you are seeking. Always make your case in a way that you use bullets to highlight certain points. Lastly, make sure your resume is submitted in a timely manner so that you are within the window of opportunity.

Cynthia Penfold reveals secrets on how to make a resume <http://www.howtomakearesumeblog.com/how-to-make-a-resume/how-to-make-a-resume-advice/> at her How To Make A Resume Blog <http://www.howtomakearesumeblog.com/>

How a Good Cover Letter Will Create Job Interviews

When apply for a job in today's market, you need to have an effective personal and attention grabbing cover letter that gets your foot in the door. Most of the job applicants simply attached a boring non-descriptive opening letter to what they hope is an outstanding resume.

This is where you can shine above your competition. Because an outstanding cover letter is not just a dust cover, but a sales letter. It's promoting your best qualities and why you should be hired over your competition. The cover letter is really a sales letter aimed at the hiring manager. It needs to stand out from the crowd and grab the attention of the hiring manager.

The fact is that a well crafted opening letter can literally be more important than your resume itself. You can have less experience and skills than your competition, but still land the job interview, simply because of your cover letter.

Most people will say to you that a good resume is the most important part of your job prospecting. But a lousy opening letter attached to a good resume will never get past the first round. The goal is to get your foot in the front door. Thus, the first document that the hiring manger will review is your cover letter. If it does not stimulate an interest in you, the hiring manager will most likely toss your resume into the trash. In a competitive job market, where you can be competing against 100-200 other job applicants, you need an edge. It's so very important to have an opening letter that grabs the attention of the hiring manager.

Therefore, you could say that the most over looked item in the job search arena is the cover letter. A narrowly focused, well crafted letter is you best bet in dramatically increasing the chance of getting that all important job interview.

Write the letter like a sales presentation. It should point out your best features and why you are the best candidate for the job. This letter is like a personal salesman, tailored to sell your benefits to the hiring manager.

For more information on how to write a killer cover letter, visit us at http://jobhuntingresources.info as well as other tips for finding that next job.

Just Say "No" to Resume Templates

When job seekers want to re-vise their resumes, or are creating them for the first time, they usually go to one standard favorite: templates from their favorite word processing software. All you have to do is fill in your person information, and you are done. Right? Not quite! Template resumes work fine for those who are not interested in distinguishing themselves from other job applicants. It might even be forgivable if you are applying for your first job and you didn't know any better. But for the rest of us, at the end of the day, there is still one rule that still applies: get creative!

What is the harm in using a template?

Templates are best used as a springboard for better ideas. When you use a template from Word (or any other software program), you are communicating the message that you aren't putting thought into your resume. Of course, what you write counts for just as much, if not more. But every resume should have its own style that echoes the message you are trying to deliver to employers. When you use a template, your work ends up looking like those of most other job applicants. It makes it tougher to leave a last impression with an employer. Aesthetics count when it comes to resumes, so make sure yours not only sounds good but looks good, too!

In addition, templates can quickly become dated if you don't upgrade your word processing software each year. Even if you do so, you still run the risk of sending a career document that will look like it was copied.

Lastly, some templates can be difficult to work with and may end up taking more time to update versus creating your own style. You don't want to spend precious time trying to figure out why extra spaces were added before certain sections, or why the bullet points aren't aligning correctly. Use your own style and you can avoid most of these kinds of headaches!

What to watch for when creating your own resume style

- Make sure to keep the look and feel of your resume appropriate for the industry, or company you would like to join. Some industries require a much more conservative look than others. For example, if you are applying for an accounting job or a job at a law firm, stick to a clean look. However, if you are in a more creative field such as fashion design or graphic design, you have more room to add flavor to your resume by adding images. When in doubt, always lean toward the more conservative side!

- Visit the web site of the company you would like to join. What kind of impression does it leave with you? If you had to sum up the web site in three or four words, what would you say? Those should be the same words one uses when they review your resume.

- Keep the style consistent throughout the resume. Consistency counts!

- Don't underestimate the value of white space. It helps make your resume much easier to read.

Interview Roadmap http://www.InterviewRoadmap.com sprung from the idea that the career documents we have (our resumes, cover letters and portfolios) create the path to landing an interview. But the right path begins with the right documents and the right type of preparation! With Interview Roadmap, you will have the right map that will get you to your ultimate destination: the interview for the job you deserve! Sherry will create the documents that land interviews, and provides the directions (interview consulting) to help you succeed once you are there.

Sherry Mirshahi, President of Interview Roadmap, has over years of experience in resume and cover letter writing, and ublic speaking. She is also a certified employment interview onsultant and her professional development includes training nd mentoring by two leading industry experts.

Visit the Interview Roadmap website ttp://www.InterviewRoadmap.com today to read about how we'll elp you land your next interview, and use the "Contact Us" page ɔ place your order.

Incorporating Your Unique Selling ʾroposition in Your Resume, Cover Letter ιnd Interviews

In part one of this article series ("Resume, Cover Letter and ιterview Makeovers Using your Unique Selling Proposition"), I ιtroduced the concept of your unique selling proposition. The rticle also explained why your USP is important, and questions ɔu should consider to find yours. In this article, you'll learn about few more ways to tap into your USP. You'll also discover how to ιcorporate it into your career documents and your interview to ιake a lasting impression with employers.

More ways to find your unique selling proposition (USP)

In trying to find your USP, first review your resume and any past cover letters you have written. If they've been written well, you'll get a good sense of some of your past accomplishments. Tapping into them will help you figure out your personal strengths. Review your performance reviews from past jobs, and any recommendations you have from past employers. These documents can also provide clues as to what you've done that has set you apart from your peers. Think about any awards you received as well! They serve as proof of your USP that you can also mention in your future interviews. Laslty, ask your friends or any past colleagues (if you stay in touch with them) if they can provide input on your strengths, accomplishments, and things you've done that have helped distinguish you professionally. Using a combination of these elements will help you find your USP quickly.

How you know you've found your USP

How do you know you have found it? It is something that feels very true for you. Your USP will be unique to you, and will provide an added dimension to everything you state in your cover letter, resume and interviews. It is the one phrase(s) that is easy to remember. Think of it as your own personal tagline. Many companies these days have communicate their USP in their taglines and advertising. Disney World is "the happiest place on earth." A Snicker's bar "really satisfies you." Bounty is the paper towel that positions itself as "the quicker picker upper." What is your personal tagline?

How to use your USP

Once you have identified your USP, you should integrate it in all of your job hunting communications. Include your USP in the body of your cover letter. Typically, you'll reserve the first paragraph for explaining which position you would like, and how you've found it. You may add in a little about yourself and include your USP then, or you may save it for the next paragraph and add in one or two examples from your career history to encourage your reader to review your resume. In your resume, add in your USP in your career summary section or your objective. During your interview, your USP is especially helpful when you integrate it into your answer for the classic question, "Tell me about yourself," or even to the question, "Where do you see yourself in five years?" Once your interview is done, be sure to include your USP again in your thank you letter, along with one or two quotes from the interview that demonstrate why you are such a good fit.

As you can see, your USP is powerful tool that will help you stay top of mind by setting you apart from other job applicants. Crafting a USP doesn't necessarily have to take very much time. However, it should be an activity in which you truly analyze where you are in your career and where you want to go in the future. Good luck!

Interview Roadmap (http://www.InterviewRoadmap.com) sprung from the idea that the career documents we have (our resumes, cover letters and portfolios) create the path to landing an interview. But the right path begins with the right documents and the right type of preparation! With Interview Roadmap, you will have the right map that will get you to your ultimate destination: the interview for the job you deserve! Sherry will create the documents that land interviews, and provides the directions (interview consulting) to help you succeed once you are there.

Sherry Mirshahi, President of Interview Roadmap, has over 5 years of experience in resume and cover letter writing, and public speaking. She is also a certified employment interview consultant and her professional development includes training and mentoring by two leading industry experts.

Visit the Interview Roadmap website (http://www.InterviewRoadmap.com) today to read about how we'll help you land your next interview, and use the "Contact Us" page to place your order.

The Problems With Resume Writing

I've read a lot of resumes in my day. Coming from the Information Technology sector I have seen some pretty crazy ones filled with a lot of gobbledygook involving technical acronyms and programming jargon.

Here's an example, "Proficient in the following languages and operating platforms: C, C++, DOS, MVS, CICS, ISPF/VS, DB2, OS/2, OS/400, AIX, UNIX, Java, JavaScript, Perl, Basic, HTML, DHTML, XHTML, XML, PHP, PDP, JCL, SQL, George 3, Win95/98/Me/XP/VISTA, etc."

Sounds pretty impressive doesn't it? The problem is verifying that the person does, in fact, know these things. Most of the time I've found they might have nothing more than a rudimentary knowledge of the subject which is why we recommend testing the applicant as opposed to just taking his/her word for it.

I also find it irritating when a person uses verbose language to describe himself. For example, whenever someone says they are a "Senior Software Engineer," this simply means he is nothing more than a programmer with two or more jobs under his belt. Some people add so many adjectives to describe their credentials and boast of their successes (not their failures) that you would think he is the second coming of Christ. Whenever I see this, I ask myself, "If this person is so great, why isn't he running his own company; why does he need a job from me?" Touting ones' successes is natural, but a little humility in the presentation of the resume would sure be refreshing.

I may not be an expert in preparing resumes, but I think the ones that appeal to me most are those that are simple and to the point. Frankly, if they cannot keep it to one page that isn't too busy looking, I think people will lose interest. I know I do. If I want additional detail, I'll ask for it. Tell me plain and simple: What are you interested in doing? What's your background? (your employment history) and What do you know? (your skill set). I don't want to know how you conquered neuro-electronic fusion systems based on a hashing algorithm you invented; do not try to baffle me with your brilliance. Just tell me how you can do a job for me and blend into the corporate culture. I think team accomplishments are still valued over individual achievement by most employers today.

Tim Bryce is a writer and management consultant located in   Palm   Harbor,   Florida. http://www.phmainstreet.com/timbryce.htm

He can be contacted at: timb001@phmainstreet.com

Essential Cover Letter Writing Tips

One of the most common mistakes which many people make when writing cover letters is to neglect the entire purpose of a cover letter. While some may go overboard with the amount and details of information they include in the letter, others, in an attempt to be informal, take an entirely-too-casual approach. It cannot be too strongly stressed that writing a cover letter is not the same as writing to a friend or a family member. Please resist the urge to be chatty, humorous, or overly personal.

The purpose of a cover letter is to provide your prospective employer with a brief view of the person who is seeking the job and the benefits and value you would bring to the company as an employee. It is meant to spark his interest in reviewing your resume and requesting an interview. The cover letter is your way of introducing yourself, making a good first impression, and outlining how you are the perfect "solution" to the employer's needs.

A good cover letter will help the prospective employer decide that he wants to know more about you, and what you can offer to his company. If you keep this in mind, you will be well on your way to writing a cover letter that does its job.

As your cover letter is the employer's first introduction to you, preparing it correctly is essential. It is a good idea to write an initial draft of the letter then "sleep on it" and review it the next day. In addition to taking care that the letter is written in the proper form for a business letter, you want to pay special attention to your spelling and grammar. One misspelled word can make the difference between capturing the employer's interest and landing your letter and resume in the "toss" pile rather than the "to interview" pile.

The information you provide in your cover letter should be clear, brief, direct, and to the point. As it is meant to be an overview of what you can bring to the company, you should focus on the most relevant facts while leaving the details for your resume. For example, if you have earned a college degree or have had prior experience that is relevant to the job, you can state these qualifications in your cover letter, but reserve dates and other specifics for your resume.

Your cover letter should inform the employer that you are interested in the job, and that you will be an asset to his company. It should let him know that you have the qualifications or experience that he is looking for in a new employee. It is your chance to make a positive impression, and to convince him that he wants to know more about you.

As one of the leading authorities on resume writing, cover letter writing <http://www.distinctiveweb.com/> , and job searching, Michelle Dumas is the founder of Distinctive Career Services LLC. Since 1996, Michelle and her team have empowered thousands of professionals worldwide with results-generating resumes, cover letters, and job search strategies. Visit http://www.distinctiveweb.com to get your free "Revive Your Resume" audio mini-seminar.

Resume Length - The Truth Hurts

You've spent your career being the A-list 'go-to' person in your department or company. Awards hang on your wall, and the company exec pops in to personally give you a 'good job' handshake every so often. You're in good standing with an admirable track record.

Does your résumé reflect that?

Most people spend the majority of their résumé space citing laundry list of what they did, rather than focusing on their accomplishments, and worrying about the length of the overall document. More importantly, they don't effectively showcase their top-line value proposition to prospective employers.

When it is not uncommon for hiring managers to receive 100, 200 and even up to 500 résumés for each open position, communicating what makes you stand out is even more critical. And résumé length has everything to do with it. The devil is in the details, and in this case, the details have to be short, sweet and to the point.

Delivering a concise, value-laden résumé takes critical editing skills. Many people end up edging past two pages once the details start to flow. This is exactly the point where the red pen needs to come out and ruthless changes need to happen. One résumé writing expert recently announced that she is now down to a one-page résumé summary for executives, who are usually the ones who flow onto three pages. (!)

So how do you winnow your background into a tidy and clear illustration about your value to prospective employers?

You need to show what you are capable of doing, not what you've done on a daily level. To get to this point, the truth hurts as you begin the editing process. A good way of thinking about it is to frame your background the following way:

Action (what you did) + Results (what was the outcome to company) = your value to the prospective employer

Take off that one responsibility that you really enjoyed but didn't produce results. Trim down extensive training and professional development classes that you've taken... leaving just the 'cherry picked' top-notch opportunities that are the most relevant to your background.

Train yourself to think about your background in terms of not what you did on a daily basis but what the overall results were to the company as a whole. Did you make them money? Save them money? Save them time? Or in the case of non-profit organizations... did you expand services? Make efficiency changes? Increase outreach and exposure?

By adopting this approach, you can drastically shorten your résumé but add focused power behind communicating what you offer to a potential employer.

It'll have an amazing effect on your viability as a candidate, and you won't be worrying about how long your résumé is at all.

Dawn Rasmussen - CTP, CMP
President
Pathfinder Writing and Career Services
PO Box 20536
Portland OR 97294
503-539-3954 phone
503-408-4894 fax
http://pathfindercareers.com/

Advance your career with a professionally - written resume!

Proud member of the National Resume Writers Association

Resume Do's and Don'ts For 2009

Creating an effective resume can be difficult for the inexperienced writer. But if you want to give it a try on your own anyway, here are a few resume writing tips and traps to consider.

Do: Think About Your Audience

When writing a resume, too many candidates think in simple terms of what tasks they performed. However, it is important to think about your resume from a strategic perspective before you write the first word. So it does not matter if you like what you put on the resume. The real question is whether those reading your resume are impressed.

So who will read my resume you ask? There are two distinct groups that you need to keep in mind: the hiring manager and the HR representative. They want to know who you worked for, what positions you have held, whether you have any employment gaps or are a frequent job hopper, and what you have accomplished.

Don't: Use an Objective Sentence

Most candidates know that you are supposed to communicate your job objective into a resume. However, most try to get fancy by writing an objective phrase or sentence that says something like, "To utilize my skills, education, and experience for a growth-oriented company." Now what does that really mean? It certainly does not tell a prospective employer what type of position you want. It tells me that you will take any job for any company that is growing, and thus not laying off it's employees. That's not a strong or confident statement. Just list your objective in the form of a title or headline. Short and simple, but effective.

Do: Include a Keywords List

Although hiring managers do not find a lot of value in a keywords list, because they are relatively meaningless, they are essential for the human resource folks, who perform word searches to generate batches of candidates for pre-screening and who compare keywords on the resume with some of the major requirements and preferences on the hiring document. Don't overwhelm the reader by listing dozens of keywords. Simply include anywhere from eight to fifteen of the terms that fit both you and the language used in the position posting.

Don't: Overuse Bullet Points

Much of the material on the market touts the effectiveness of a bulleted format in a resume. This is largely true. However, many people end up burying some of their key highlights because they list every single thought next to a bullet. Make sure you put your basic job duties in paragraph-style text so that you can reserve the bullets for the items you want to showcase like cost-savings initiatives, sales results, performance metrics, and key projects managed.

Following these do's and don'ts will help improve the look, readability, and impact that your resume has with both HR reps and hiring managers.

So who am I anyway? Why do I think my advice is so valuable?

My name is Stephen Van Vreede. My company is called No Stone Unturned, and I have spent 15 years on both sides of the corporate hiring experience.

The short story is that I have an MBA in Marketing from Villanova University and a dual B.S. degree in Finance & Logistics from the University of Maryland. I am a certified professional résumé writer (CPRW) and a member of the Professional Association of Résumé Writers and Career Coaches (PARW/CC). As I mentioned, I paid my dues in the corporate world eventually running a large-scale call center for a major truck rental company, and I have spent the past 7 years with No Stone Unturned, assisting job seekers in achieving their goals.

In February 2009, I launched a new group job hunting networking site: NoddlePlace.com. It is absolutely FREE to join, and you have access to everything on the site. Come check it out at NoddlePlace <http://www.noddleplace.com> . You can also follow me on Twitter <http://www.twitter.com/noddleplace> .

Darn Good Reasons Why You Should Or Should Not Hire A Professional Resume Service

Well, if you live in Michigan, or anywhere else in our country, let's face it. The economy stinks. People are getting laid off and companies are closing down or outsourcing to other countries practically on a daily basis. So, what good would hiring a professional resume service do for you? EVERYTHING.

It's understandable to be cautious about hiring a resume writer, especially online where you can't visually shake a hand or see an office full of certificates, awards, books, or anything else that might prove credibility. Here are a few reasons you SHOULD hire a professional resume writer:

1- PROFESSIONALISM - A professional resume writer knows what he/she is doing. I've had clients tell me over and over that having it professionally written got them the job. They had sent in the old one previously and at my urging, resent the new one and got the job!

Make sure whomever you hire is CERTIFIED. If you are unsure whether or not your writer is certified, go to parw.com and type in their name. If they are certified, it will come up as such. A certified writer has gone through extensive training and was tested on it, ensuring their work meets the standards of the Professional Association of Resume Writers and Career Coaches. If you are going to spend the money, you want the best.

2- BRANDING/PR - A professional resume writer acts as our personal cheerleader, your brander, your public relations irm. You want someone who knows how to present your qualifications in your best light. They will gather the relevant information career goals, experience, training, etc.) to create a professional nage for you. Something you will be proud to hand out to a hiring nanager.

3-GHOSTWRITERS- A professional resume writer knows ow to craft content that gets people interested. They create a esume that sounds and feels like YOU. A professional resume vriter constantly updates their skills and abilities by keeping up vith the latest in career news, and attending webinars, telesemi-ars and conferences.

4- FORMAT - How bored are you when you see a resume hat is bullet after bullet of a position description? Would you call hat person back? Neither will the hiring person. Professional esume writers are TRAINED in creating unique documents with ppealing fonts, borders and styling that is all YOU.

5- RESOURCE CENTER - Your professional resume writer s a career one-stop-shop! Chances are they have a wide range of esources to offer during your job search. Many are also Certified 'areer Coaches and remain well informed of career events and ther services helpful to their clients. Many times employers will ontact resume writers for suitable candidates.

Reasons NOT TO HIRE a professional resume writer:

1- They offer you a resume package for $19.95. Most likely his company is a printing or secretarial service that will rewrite verything you gave them, or dump your info into a pre-written emplate.

2- They tell you they are certified, but you check on the 'ARW site and they are not. WRONG. Turn around and go back. 'hey are misrepresenting the truth and God knows what they will o with your money.

3- They offer a 30-day guarantee if you don't get an interview. I know this is a touchy one, because many of my colleagues do it, but here is my beef with that: with each client, I put my heart and soul into the resume. I am already writing a resume that I think will knock the socks off any reader. So how can I possibly offer a rewrite on that? I already wrote a killer resume and I stand behind it. I would rather sit down with the client and go over what they have been doing for job search because I guarantee that is where the problems lie.

So, to sum it up, it's important to find a solid and reputable resume service. Check for memberships to professional career organizations with writers that are certified.

A professionally written resume is a good investment and is worth it's weight in gold, not to mention it will get you noticed immediately.

Erin Kennedy is a Certified Professional & Executive Resume Writer & Career Consultant, and President of Professional Resume Services. She is a Nationally Published Writer & Contributor in 8 best selling career books. Erin has achieved the prestigious T.O.R.I. (Toast of the Resume Industry) Award nomination in 2007 and 2008.

To get more career-related information and resume writing tips, visit Professional Resume Services at http://www.proreswriters.com or check out her blog at: proreswriters.blogspot.

Creative. Powerful. Proven.

Erin is a member of: Professional Association of Resume Writers (PARW), Career Directors International (CDI), Association of Online Resume and Career Professionals (AORCP), Career Professionals Group, and Women for Hire.

Want to know more about Erin Kennedy, CPRW? Read her LinkedIn profile at: http://www.linkedin.com/in/erinkennedycprw

Essential Resume Writing Tips That You Must Know

For many people, the thought of writing a resume can be confusing and even intimidating. Whether you have recently graduated from college, or whether you have been in the workforce for many years and are looking for a new and better job, having a properly prepared resume is essential for your success. Your resume is your prospective employer's first view of you--it must convince him that you are the person he should hire for the job.

When writing their own resumes, many people make either of two mistakes. Either they provide too much information, or they do not provide enough. As your prospective employer is busy, it is unwise to go overboard with too much information, the wrong kinds of information, and unnecessary details. Similarly, as he needs to know exactly what your qualifications are, being too modest about your accomplishments and other relevant facts will not be in your favor.

The best resume will tell your prospective employer what you can bring to the job and what you can offer to the company itself. The information you include on your resume should be clear and brief. While there are a number of different formats of resumes, whichever resume format you choose the most important rule is that your resume be absolutely accurate and truthful. You will need to provide the names of your previous employers, and the dates during which you worked for each company. You will also need the names and dates of your college attendance. As various other types of experiences are an asset in job searching, relevant experiences in community service, school organizations, and other accomplishments can also be included on your resume.

As you are competing against hordes of other job searchers, and your resume is often the single most important factor in whether you get a call for an interview, professional resume writing may be the answer for you. This is the best way to ensure that your resume is in the correct form suitable for the job you are seeking, and that it is prepared properly with a focus on accomplishments and the value that you offer to the workplace.

Today's job market is much more competitive than ever before. Regardless of your level of skills, qualifications, education and prior work experience, having as much as possible in your favor when job searching will increase your chance of success. When you have your resume prepared by a professional, you are giving yourself the best possible edge over the competition.

As one of the leading authorities on resume writing, cover letter writing <http://www.distinctiveweb.com/> , and job searching, Michelle Dumas is the founder of Distinctive Career Services LLC. Since 1996, Michelle and her team have empowered thousands of professionals worldwide with results-generating resumes, cover letters, and job search strategies. Visit http://www.distinctiveweb.com to get your free "Revive Your Resume" audio mini-seminar.

The 7 Secrets to Resume Writing and Business Success

I was asked on a radio show what are the real secrets to getting a job in this economy. With so many people looking for employment, you must insure that your resume stands out. There are 7 secrets that will insure that you are the star that your future employer plucks out of the sky. Remember that the goal of a resume is to get an interview, so take a leadership stance and total personal responsibility to make it a great one.

1. What is your job objective? You can't scribe before this step. This is your hook, and the statement that most people don't even consider. It is the key that gets you noticed. And always write it from the employer's point of view.

Self-serving objective: To obtain a responsible (as opposed to irresponsible?) and challenging (what, you don't like dull work?) position where my education and work experience will have valuable application (like finding a cure for cancer?)

Attention-getting objective: Mid-level management position in sales where over 10 years of experience will add value to the sales department and company profits.

2. Companies now scan your resume and will look for key words. Pay close attention to the posting of the job and use their words that have been chosen by the hiring manager. If you use paragraphs, your resume will wind up in the circular file. Chose bullet points for your concise statements. You should always use %'s, $'s and #'s. Percentages, dollar totals, and numbers stand out in the body of a resume.

Incorrect: Was the top sales producer for the region

Correct: Managed 20% of all accounts with sales in excess of $20M annually

3. Customize your resume for each company. This will increase your chance of an interview and remember - that is the goal! It's all about personal responsibility, and self-leadership for you to find your business success.

4.   Read a book about graphic design. Look at ads and pay attention to where you look first. Design is important on your resume! Open space or "white space" is good. Font should be no smaller than 10 point and use Times New Roman or a similar style.

5.   Stay upbeat and positive. There is no room for toxic behavior and negative stories. If you don't want there to be an issue with your age, do not include your year of graduation. Remember this also when listing your positions and companies.

6.   Focus only on what is relevant to the job you are seeking. Leave off irrelevant information such as race, gender, and other personal statistics. Have someone else read and critique your resume with specific examples of why it is good or bad. You are way to close to be objective. Remember to limit the resume to one page!

7.   Choose a high quality of 24-pound cream or white colored paper on which to print your resume. Consider water marked paper and envelopes. Make sure the envelope is well formatted, the return address is clear and even check that the stamp is square in the corner. It is all about first impression.

Now that your resume is done, email me for your copy of The Ten Commandments of Cooperation so your interview rewards you with a job offer!

———————————

Marsha Petrie Sue, MBA, CSP - Decontaminator of Toxic People - Professional Speaker and Author

Featured in the New York Times, Business Journal, Investors Business Digest, Legal Management, WorkWise and more.

Author of Toxic People: Decontaminate Difficult People at Work without Using Weapons or Duct Tape and The CEO of YOU: Leading Yourself to Success - Translated into Russian, Romanian and French by John Wiley - New York

Booking information: 1.888.797.6700
View   Demo:
ıttp://www.youtube.com/watch?v=fgPaiX7exm4

"Silence is Golden. Duct Tape is Silver."
Website http://www.MarshaPetrieSue.com

How To Write A Winning CV

1. MAKE USE OF ALL AVAILABLE SPACE AND FORMATTING

A good graduate Curriculum Vitae should not exceed 2 pages. Research proves that no more than 48% of interviewers read past page 1. In other words, if you CV is 2 pages make sure you have all the important stuff (e.g. what makes YOU stand out) in the first page and treat page 2 as more of an annex. If the recruiter does not read it, no big deal.

Having said this, you can put a LOT of information in one page. Use tables in word, they are an easy way of making good use of space while making sure that everything is aligned as it should be. It is impressive the number of CVs that have grey boxes, lines, double lines, etc. Always ask yourself: how do they help you stand out? They don't.

They only take precious recruiter attention away from the facts that make you a top candidate.

2. USE STANDARD FONTS AND COLOURS, PDF IF POSSIBLE

Arial or Times New Roman work best, white background with white text. No fancy animations. Many people (especially at interview stage) will print the CV on paper therefore any non-standard colours and animations will not come through and will make the CV look odd.

If you are sending your resume in electronic format try sending it in PDF format rather than MS Word if possible. It looks much more professional and you are guaranteed that the layout on the receiving end will be what you want it to be.

3. MAKE SURE THERE ARE NO TYPOS, SPELLING ERRORS, ETC

Any of those errors would get your CV straight into the trash a good 90% of the time. The interviewer would think: "If you didn't bother taking 2 minutes to spell check your CV before applying why should I hire you and spend months training you?"

C'mon, you have spell check tools everywhere - how on earth can you have a mistake on your resume?

Make sure all formatting is consistent. Example, if you say you studied in "Berlin, Germany" then you need to use the same [City], [Country] format anywhere else in the CV

CONCLUSION

Your CV is your business card. You have days, weeks, months to prepare it. You can ask for help either from friends, family or professionals. There is NO reason on earth why it should not be outstanding. The two primary reasons for rejection at entry-level positions (i.e. graduate level)

1.   Simple mistakes that prove lack of preparation and attention to detail

2.   Not having in mind what the recruiter wants to know and instead dumping dates and degrees and waiting for the interviewer to decipher them and work out why you are the best candidate.

Following these tips will get you a long long way into landing the job offer, with little effort.

Agustin Valecillos is a Vice President at a top tier Investment bank focussing on Commodities and FX Structuring. He is also the Founder and CEO of a team of Investment Banking professionals who pride themselves in helping people jump-start their   investment   banking   career <http://www.helpmegetajob.co.uk>   in   the   financial   services sector through an outstanding banking CV, cover letter and application   form.   For   the   latest   techniques,   visit http://www.helpmegetajob.co.uk

Find a Job - Step 7 - Crafting a Value Proposition Idea Letter, VPI

By now, you should have read the first six articles on finding a job and you understand the importance of a Value Proposition Idea (VPI). You may, however, be wondering why you are going to put this in the form of a letter?   It's important for you do something to get yourself on the radar screen of the decision-maker. The prior research that you preformed may have yielded some very important insight into problem areas that you can offer solutions for. It does you no good if you don't get your ideas in front of the right people.

Your Value Proposition Idea (VPI) letter can be submitted as an e-mail, voicemail or snail mail; they all work. A VPI letter functions as the cover letter in a traditional resume, with two marked differences. Cover letters typically don't get read, and more importantly, they are all about you. As a result, they are generally quite ineffective. You will recall we covered the importance of making this entire exercise about the decision-maker. The Value Proposition Idea (VPI) letter is designed to do that and can deliver startling results. The surprising thing is that the VPI letter consists of only three short paragraphs. A point of caution, don't make the mistake of dumping your life in the VPI letter; nothing will get you shot down faster!

VPI Letter Outline

Paragraph 1- Passion or Referral- here you do one or both of two things; either you explain your passion for the industry and the company or reference a referral you might have, "Mr. Jones suggested that I contact you. " Above all, be passionate, that is very important.

Paragraph 2- VPI Highlights-here you are going to talk a little bit about what your idea or solution embodies. As an example, "I've got this idea for a possible new product rollout that addresses the current issue in the market and the potential profits are in the $10 million range." (the more compelling the better.)

Paragraph 3- Contact Information-paragraph 3 is very short. It simply states, "If you are interested in discussing this idea, I can be reached at _____" Give your phone number and e-mail. Finally, you just sign the note. Do not include a title, letterhead or anything else, just your name. You want to convey a bit of mystery.

You might want to consider sending a similar letter to the competitors of the company. Here's the crucial point. Rather than sending them an e-mail with a resume hoping to land an interview, you have done research to identify problem issues that the decision-maker is desirous of solving. You may have gathered insight consulting with your High Impact Advisory Team for potential solutions (remember, we covered the HIAT back in the Step 3 article).

Here's the point I want to make about the VPI Letter. This is the first time you are making contact with the decision-maker and yet you are talking about their industry, you have identified hot-button issues he or she is interested in and are offering potential solutions. Here is a suggestion about what to put in the subject line of the e-mail. I would recommend something regarding the problem or issue your research has identified, that the decision-maker is interested in. This gets their attention and raises their curiosity. The more pain their problem is causing them, the more urgency they will feel to contact you. Most people e-mail their resumes to the universe stating that they saw there was a job opening and suggest they are the one to fill it. Do you see how this is radically different this approach is? It's not just radical, it really works. You do this process with three or four of your targeted companies and prepare to be amazed at the results. Is not uncommon for the decision-maker to contact you the same day!

What do you do when they contact you indicating they want to speak to you about your e-mail? Now we are going to prepare for the VPI Briefing, but that's the subject of our next article!

Find A Job- Step 8, The VPI Briefing

Dennis Whitlock has enjoyed a varied career in both the profit and not for profit fields. He has been a National Sales Director for a Fortune 500 company, founded and operated a successful medical service company for nearly 20 years and, most recently, been a founding partner in Verax, LLC. a sales and marketing company using social medial on the internet to drive business in the New Economy. He lives with his wife Susan and their two sons outside of Denver, Colorado.

Incredible Secrets of a One Page Resume That Will Score the Interview & Land the Job You Really Want

The first page of your resume is the most important. You have only a few seconds to grab the reader's attention and convince them that you're qualified for the job. If you haven't convinced them by the end of Page One, they'll probably never get to Page Two.

I've been getting a lot of requests for one-page resumes lately. Even though it is not a requirement that a resume be one page, many applicants think that it gives them an edge in the job search.

The truth is that anything -- and everything -- that relates to the specific job requirements needs to be on the first page. Preferably, it should be in top third or top half of the first page.

In the past, you could make the connection between your qualifications and the job requirements in a cover letter. However, it's very difficult to include a cover letter when submitting a resume online.

Here's how to combine your resume with a cover letter and do it in one page:

1. Make a list of the job requirements.

Turn each requirement into to a two- to four-word description. For example, if they "require one to two years experience in the hospitality industry," you'll write "Hospitality Experience" or "Hospitality Industry Experience."

2. Make a list of your qualifications.

For each requirement, write one or two sentences about your qualification. Something like "3+ years of Hospitality experience as front-of-house manager."

If possible, use examples. Examples sell. For instance: "Wrote employee training manual" is much better than "Excellent written communications skills."

3. List the requirements and qualifications side-by-side.

Make a two-column table on the top of your resume. Put the requirements on the left (filling 1/3 of the page width) and your qualifications on the right (filling 2/3 of the page width). No column headings are needed.

List as many requirements/qualifications as will fit in the top half of the page.

4. List your experience and education.

You only need to go back 7 to 10 years. You can go back further if the experience is really, really relevant to the position.

This part will be a balancing act. If you've held a lot of positions, you may not be able to describe a lot about each one, or you'll need to go over to a second page. If you've worked for only a few companies, then you'll be able to describe each job more fully.

Ready to learn more about how to get more interviews <http://www.magneticresume.com> for each resume you send out?

Download my FREE 12-page report, "Anatomy of a Perfect Resume," at http://www.magneticresume.com so you can learn:

* The 4 most common deadly mistakes that people make and how to fix them!
* How to create the perfect Career Objective & Career Summary sections
* How to maximize your resume so you're the candidate your next boss wants to meet!

Scott Shane Holt has seen it all while hiring over 100 people, in good times and bad, and as an executive coach helping managers and other professionals accelerate their careers.

What Will it Take? Is Someone Going to Read Your Resume?

Cover Letters

The cover letter for a job application is now considered to be a part of the job application. That's a fair assessment, because the cover letter has a lot of possible uses for job applicants.

The modern job market is looking for "fits" for people and jobs. It also wants motivated people. A CV or resume can indicate objectives, or skills, but it can't convey personal enthusiasm very well. Nor can it include extra information like quality of experience, beyond fairly basic work history.

The cover letter is a method of expression, above all else. That can be the difference between getting a job and not getting an interview.

Cover letter basics

A cover letter should be one page, preferably. Try to stick to that as the basic benchmark for size. If you absolutely must include more, keep it brief and to the point.

The most important thing about a cover letter is that it can provide additional information to an employer. Define your message well. You're telling the employer what you want them to know beyond the information they already have from your application.

? If you're enthusiastic about a job: Say so!
? Use your career path as a guide for the reader: "I want this job as part of my goal to become..."

? If you have special experience, mention it, in context with your motivation. This can be anything from a particular professional reference to personal experience nobody else has.

Drafting your cover letter

The steps of drafting a cover letter might look a lot for a one page letter, but they're all necessary:

? What do you want to tell the employer?
? What do you need to tell the employer?
? What information do you have that's obviously useful to your application, but isn't contained in your CV or resume?
? How to express your information?

If that also looks like an editing process, you're quite right.

? What you want to tell the employer is what the employer needs to hear: You're motivated, and you have practical reasons for your application, in the form of your career goals.
? What the employer wants to hear is what the employer is trying to find: Value. You're telling the employer you can add value.
? The information you have that isn't contained in your application is your strong suit: Your personality, and personal commitment. If you're after a position you really want, that's easy enough to do in a cover letter.

Now we come to the tricky bit:

How to express your information? This is a business letter. Your business, and the employer's. It should be written like a business letter.

The phraseology varies with each individual, but you know what a business letter should look like:

? It must look professional.
? It must contain useful information.
? It must have a good, unique, stand out style.

Job applications are highly competitive. You may be one of a thousand people going for a job. The cover letter is part of your application. Others going for the job may have similar skills, but they won't write the same cover letter.

Draft your letter. What's wrong with it? Does it say what you want it to say? Does it look professional, or like something you wrote at 3AM on the last day to lodge the application?

One basic rule: If it doesn't look good enough, it isn't. Try again.

Result: A good cover letter. And now you know you've got it right.

Your cover letter can get you a job. Make it do that.

At examplesof.com/cover_letter you will find the different types of cover letters <http://www.examplesof.com/cover_letter/> which will help you in writing your cover letter and making it more effective and attractive. For more info please visit http://www.examplesof.com/cover_letter/

Resume Cover Letters - What Do You Need to Include?

A resume cover letter is a letter that we send mostly when are applying for a job. It provides additional information about us and also highlights our special interest in that job. A good resume cover letter shows how our unique background fits the needs of the company that advertises the job we are interested in. This letter must be made to align with our job profile and the needs of the job as well.

The structure of a resume cover letter follows a certain pattern. You must begin by writing your address details (name, city, country, area code number, telephone number and e-mail address). The date comes next and the details of the employer (title, department, employer's name and address). Then an opening formula containing the name of the employer (if known) should follow.

The first paragraph must contain the reason you are writing for. Here you must include the very position you are applying for and where exactly you have heard of it. If there is any mutual contact, it is a good idea to mention his or her name; your cover letter will get more chances to be read through if you do.

The style in which you are writing is very important. You must show how passionate and enthusiastic you are about the prospect of being chosen to work for that company; that will make a good impression for sure.

In the body of your resume cover letter you are supposed to show why you are a desirable candidate for the position in question. Here you are expected to give details on your qualifications that you have written about in your resume and try convincing the reader that you are the best choice for the job that has been advertised. Be explicit and bring arguments to sustain the idea that your qualifications really meet the job requirements. Any achievements that you had in the past must be mentioned in this part of the cover letter as well as your special ability to solve problems. The body is usually made up of two paragraphs, with your eligibility for the job plus a list of skills and abilities in the first paragraph and some points about your qualities that are not mentioned in the

esume but make you better than any other competent in the
econd.

The final paragraph of the resume cover letter is where you
irectly ask for an interview, being very specific about the time
hat you are available for it. You should also give any details about
vhere you can be reached so that the employer may do that with-
ut to much trouble (phone number and e-mail address will do).
)on't forget to be polite and thank the employer for taking a
noment to read your cover letter and resume.

A polite closing formula will end the resume cover letter,
vith your signature and full name typed.

Remember to be as explicit and concise as possible without
verlooking the natural fluency that makes a letter readable. The
orm in which you address a potential employer is the first step
owards getting a chance for an interview.

To get more help with writing resume cover letters
http://www.squidoo.com/how-to_make_a_resume>   just go
ere <http://www.squidoo.com/how-to_make_a_resume> .

What Job Resume Format Should You Jse?

A job resume is a concise document presenting your most relevant credentials for employment. It is meant, just like a cover letter, to get you an interview (not a job).

When you start devising your resume, you must keep one very important thing in mind: on average, an employer will spend less than one minute to read through your resume, which means it must not be longer than one page. Of course, the style and length of a resume differs from country to country and from company to company. East Europeans and Americans tend to be more concise than applicants in Western Europe who would gladly fill over two pages with (unimportant) detailed information.

There is a good explanation for the uselessness of a long resume; an employer knows if you are worth the time for an interview if he or she casts a quick glance at your resume and cover letter. Any details may be gone into later. As for the specific format that a resume should have, there are several formats available, which means there is room for creativity, but the necessary information must be there in a logical order in each of them.

The most common type of resume is called 'chronological'. It lists your education as well as experience in reverse chronological order. Thus, your most recent activity must be listed first. Of course, there are variations in which you can use headings that highlight your background and qualifications but otherwise there is nothing special about them.

Another job resume format that people use is one that concentrates on the skills, grouping the various experiences that you have had according to the skills necessary to each of them.

Whichever style of job resumes you may choose there is certain information that must be there: permanent and current address (if different), objective (the type of job you are after), education (usually latest school first), computer skills (this is very important nowadays in all fields of activity), experience and activity (in reverse chronological order, as mentioned above), honours and distinctions (if any) and, of course, availability.

A few employers expect a scannable resume which is a document that can be scanned as a graphic image and then converted back to text - a rather strict format which does not allow you to be very creative while typing that kind of resume; on the contrary, you must stick to certain rules and guidelines: you are not allowed to use italics, bold, all caps, underlining or shading; only sans serif fonts are acceptable; equal size is a must; no bullets, no horizontal and vertical lines, no boxes or graphics, no tabs either, only even spacing throughout the document and the list may go on with a long series of do's and don'ts. On top of that, you must use a laser printer and provide the employer with the original or a high-quality photocopy. If you think you may need such a resume, you had better search the web for more details about it.

To get more help on how to make a job resume <http://www.squidoo.com/how-to_make_a_resume> just go here <http://www.squidoo.com/how-to_make_a_resume> .

Tips For Maximizing the Effectiveness of Your Resume

Regardless of whether you are entering the workforce for the first time, or going back to work after a long absence, there are several elements related to your return to the workforce to consider. At the top of the list is your choice of resume formats. There are three resume formats used in business today. The different types of formats are: Chronological, Functional and Combination.

Among the most popular formats is the chronological resume, which emphasizes, in a very structured order, your work
history. Chronological resumes list your job history in reverse
order starting with your most recent or present job, followed by
the job or position you held immediately prior to your most recent
or current job, which is followed by the once before that, and so
on. Typically, this type of resume lists the history of your last 10
years of jobs, job descriptions and job titles. These types of resumes are best suited for entry-level job seekers or those who have
remained in the same industry for a long period. If however, you
are interested in a career change and you have a variety of work
experience, you may want to consider using a 'functional' resume,
instead.

Candidates wanting to highlight special accomplishments
use functional style resumes. If you are going to opt for this style
of resume, your resume will be far more effective if you list your
accomplishments in bullet form. Functional resumes are also used
when you do not have a lot of career-related experience but can
identify the skills that you proven and become proficient and that
can be transferred from one job or industry to another. It is also
important to remember that any skills learned while doing volunteer work is relevant and important to list where applicable.

Combination resumes, also known as hybrid resumes, are
most suited for job seekers with long work-histories or people with
special skills and a strong record of accomplishments. Combination resumes combine the best of the chronological and the functional resumes. This hybrid allows you to highlight choice skills
and accomplishments while downplaying your past employers, job
titles and the amount of time you spent in each position.

Regardless of your choice of resume format, it is critical
that your resume be as 'scannable' as possible. It is important to
know that most large companies and recruiting firms now use
Optical Character Recognition [OCR] software to identify and
extract information from resumes and cover letters that are submitted electronically. In addition to your basic contact information, i.e. name, address, and phone number, et cetera, the software
will search for specific keywords. It is vital that regardless of the

resume format you choose, industry keywords need to be embedded in both your cover letter and resume in order to be effective. Resumes that are poorly written and use non-standard formats will not be scanned correctly and reduce your chances of getting interviews.

How to Maximize Scannability:

* Use white 8 ½ x 11 paper

* Avoid folding or using stables

* Use a standard font [New Times Roman, Arial, or Courier]

* Use standard font size [12-14 points]

* Use spacing between lines sensibly

* Place contact information on each page of your resume

How to Maximize Resume Hits:

* Use keywords that are specific to the industry
* Avoid using jargon and spell out acronyms
* Use concrete descriptors when listing your experience

By choosing the appropriate resume for your needs and combining it with the tips on how to make your resume 'scannable', your chances of getting calls for interviews will increase substantially. If you do not feel that you have the necessary wordsmith skills to have an impact, there is nothing wrong with asking for help. Good luck!

©Salvino011809

Mary Salvino MBA is a freelance writer and career/business consultant who lives in Vancouver, BC. She has many years of experience in all aspects of career and business management. Mary is also a valuable resource to both corporations and individuals in the area of marketing and strategic planning.

Cover Letter Examples - Available on the Internet

There are lots of cover letter examples to choose from - internet websites offer a lot of these. Mostly, information about the previous job of the applicant is written in it. Cover letter examples are only the guide since it must consist of the things that reflect your skills, training and experiences. Also, this could tell the readers about your personality and attitude and how it is matched to the job that you are applying for.

Look for cover letter examples where in the objectives, reasons for applying for that certain job and the interest of the applicant are present. This is actually a relevant tool in creating cover letters in many ways. Put in mind that you should take time to review the examples that you have, and then make sure that your cover letter gives a profound explanation on your skills and how it is related to the job criteria that are listed. Remember that this is a letter of purpose; you need to do it well and construct it seriously. This letter will be send to the company that the applicant is applying for with a certain proposal, a resume for job application is a good example of such, and aside from this, it provides some added information on the job interests of the applicant and of course those job interests should be high lighted too.

In writing a cover letter, be sure to write it in complete uniqueness, the background of it should fit in the company's needs and should make the recruiter or the HR personnel to call you and set an interview. Be sure that your cover letter will be aligned with your profile and the job needs.

Margaret Marquisi is a retired writer and full time grand-
mother. To learn more about cover letter examples
<http://www.coverlettersthatkill.com> or cover letter samples
<http://www.coverlettersthatkill.com>, visit her website.

How Do You Properly Write Your Resume?

You may be the best employee in the world, but if you can
not write a good resume you will probably never find your dream
job. The corporate world puts a lot of emphasis on resumes. Your
resume is essentially your first impression. So if your resume is
put together improperly and filled with fluff instead of substance
you will never even get your foot in the door.

The first thing you need to decide is if you are able to write
your own resume properly. If you have been sending your resume
out and receiving no responses then there is a good chance you are
not sending out a quality resume. If that is the case you may want
to seek professional help to produce a quality resume for you.

Secondly, keep your resume short and sweet. Most employers will only be scanning the first page of your resume; so if you
turn in a resume with multiple pages of accomplishments they will
probably never be seen. You want to list the most important
details quickly and precisely so you can get your foot in the door.

Then you can always talk about your accomplishments in more detail once you get an actual interview.

Thirdly, keep your resume real. If you pretend to know more than you actually do you will not only be wasting the employers time, but your time as well. It is not hard to figure out when a potential employee is in over their head.

Lastly, keep your resume clean. This means do not use fancy colored paper or wild fonts when creating your resume. Many companies will scan resumes by machine to find trigger words and phrases before they ever actually read them. This helps companies quickly go through many resumes at a time to weed out the bad ones without wasting human labor. Therefore, you need to keep your resume layout simple so it can be easily read by machines.

Chad Surges has a Bachelor's Degree in Business and currently owns and operates the investing website called lucky-dog-investing.com <http://www.lucky-dog-investing.com> . He also invites you to visit his job network website: chiob.com

Writing a Resume Cover Letter - 3 Essential Questions to Outline Your Letter of Intent

When you're finally done with your resume, the next step is writing a resume cover letter. If it's a daunting task to write your resume, it is twice more daunting to write a cover letter. Why? Since this will be the first one to look for in a resume, the idea of creating an impression primarily is important. Even if a cover letter is just a one-page concise and brief statement weigh against numbers of pages of your resume, cover letters still stands as the far more complicated type of letter to put in paper.

Writing a resume cover letter need not have expertise in words, it need not have pompous, big and flowery statements, rather what it should mainly exhibit are simple sentences that make sense and are interrelated with each other.

To give you a glimpse of the following key factors to comprise your resume cover letter, here are the following guidelines.

What is the Position You're Applying For?

Indicate the desired and particular position you're applying for, first and foremost. Your cover letter should consist of the job title you want to get into. Do not suppose that employers have a solid idea of the purpose of your letter of intent, so you better be specific in your objectives. There are times when there are numerous job postings in a particular company and it would be hard for the person in charge to discern which is which since no indication is made. Therefore, to steer clear of confusions and in finding your hard work curriculum vitae in the trash, you need to take proper consideration in designating your concern.

How Do You Find Out About the Vacancy?

Another significant aspect to include in your curriculum vitae cover letter is the question, 'How do you find out of the job and the company'? Your grounds can be stated in your cover letter and this can include the options of an online source, newspapers job postings and other media advertisements or a referral from an employee of the company itself. It is important to note these down for both the benefit of the applicant and the management as well. For the applicant for further notes and points about the company and for the company to discern which hiring advertisements work for them best.

How Do You Create a Formal and Efficient Resume Cover Letter?

Writing a resume cover letter should have 12 point font size with appropriate spaces in between words, sentences and paragraphs. Avoid overcrowding and overstuffing of words and sentences - this will only create an unprofessional and unpleasant cover letter. Apart from this, you also need to avoid including graphics and other icons that is not significant in your letter of intent. Rather make it a kind of letter that is easy to read and understand.

Mark Mattey is a writer and entrepreneur. To learn more about writing a resume cover letter <http://www.coverlettersthatkill.com> or cover letter templates <http://www.coverlettersthatkill.com> , visit his website.

A Quick Guide on Cover Letter Format

First things first, what is a cover letter? A cover letter is your way to be able to introduce yourself to the person who will be interviewing you in such a way that there is no need for you to give out a long monologue of your family history, academic background, and work experience. A cover letter, to put it simply, is where you will be able to put in your career objectives in the company, this is your way of letting the interviewer know how interested you are in working for their company and how passionate you are about the available position.

To be able to do this you need to have the right cover letter format, there are a lot of people who just babble on and on in their cover letters and this can be quite a turn off for interviewers as they are not really interested in the nitty gritty details of the applicants' lives. What they really want to learn about is how effective you will be for the company and how will you be able to communicate that to your interviewer? Through the right cover letter format of course!

For the right cover letter format that will help you pique the interest of the interviewer to consider your job or internship application, keep the language of your letter formal yet not too stiff. Just simply show the interviewer your professionalism by giving a letter that is business-like but don't forget to make sure that you are able to send your point across. Be very clear with your motives and be able to impress the interviewer in your genuine interest in working in the company. Also, always be mindful to highlight your key skills that will prove to be an asset for the job or internship that you are applying for.

Mark Mattey is a writer and entrepreneur. To learn more about cover letter format <http://www.coverlettersthatkill.com> or coverletter templates & examples <http://www.coverlettersthatkill.com> , visit his website.

Fresh Grad? - Make Use of Cover Letter Examples

Have you recently graduated? If so, then you are one of the many young ones who are all eager to get their first jobs. While job hunting can end as short as a few days or as long as many months, you can actually make the process of job hunting easy and effective by making only the best impressions. If you believe that you are qualified for the job that you have applied for, then do not let your abilities and efforts be wasted with a wrongfully written cover letter and resume. Do not let all your credentials go down the drain simply because you do not know how to write an impressive cover letter. Cover letter examples are now available online and you can have access to these powerful cover letters easily.

Cover letter examples are made available online to guide those who o not know how to write killer cover letters. Since the competition for jobs are ever increasing, it has become necessary that you have perfectly written cover letters in order to send the best possible impression to the companies that you have applied for. Do not waste your time making a cover letter of your own if you have zero knowledge on how to write it. You will just inflict more damage. Make use of impressive cover letter examples so you do not leave your job hunting success to chance.

Even if you are a fresh graduate, you can land that dream job you want. All you need is a powerful cover letter to make any company call you back for an interview. Making the right impressions at the right time gives you the edge over the hundreds of other applicants.

Mark Mattey is a writer and entrepreneur. To learn more about cover letter examples <http://www.coverlettersthatkill.com> or cover letter templates & examples <http://www.coverlettersthatkill.com> , visit his website.

Writing a Cover Letter - Crucial Tips to Remember When Writing a Cover Letter

Writing a cover letter means you're ready to face the world f employment and job opportunities. However, don't be like a lone and copy a basic format off the Internet. Instead, make it 1ore interesting and personalized.

You don't have to use scented papers or those with crazy olors when writing a cover letter. In all honesty, what's important ; the content. Below are some useful tips:

1) Keep it simple.

When writing a cover letter, keep in mind all the important oints about yourself. What makes you stand out from the rest of 1e applicants? What are your strengths and assets? Include these 1 it and you'll have a better chance of receiving a call from the ompany.

2) Check your grammar.

A cover letter is not like a resume and is written in para- raphs. If you're not very well-versed in the English language, it's est to have others double check it for any errors. Any grammati- al error or typo automatically turns the employers off, so beware.

3) Use company details.

Employers like it when they see that the applicant has done is or her research. When writing a cover letter, you have to keep 1 mind the questions which are likely running around in your interviewer's head. Why should they hire you? What do you have that the company needs? Always think in terms of the company you're applying for and include it in your cover letter.

Writing a cover letter can make or break the deal. Don't think of it as just another piece of paper that your employer will toss into the trash can. Most employers actually read it first before proceeding onto the resume. If your cover letter has too many errors and does not interest the boss, then don't expect them to take a look at your resume either. And that would kill any chances of you getting the job.

Want to get your dream job? Get FREE tips and video on how to write a cover letter <http://www.squidoo.com/how-to-write-a-cover-letter-for-a-resume> that grabs attention like a magnet, and secrets of preparing for a job interview <http://www.20daypersuasion.com/job-interview.htm> that gets you hired on the spot.

Cover Letters - When Applying For a Job

Cover letters are actually important pages that should be given time and effort when applying for a job. Getting a job in a good and reputable company is becoming more and more difficult by the day due to the recession that has been going on for the past few months, so it's pretty obvious that the standards and qualificaions of potential employees have risen even higher than ever before. If you really want to grab their attention and snag that interview invitation, then the first thing to work on first is your cover letter.

The cover letter goes along with your resume when you submit it to the HR manager/s of the company. It is usually the first page they see when they begin browsing through your resume, which basically addresses them in a professional way and informs them of your interest in the position that the company is opening up to the public. Now the reason why it is important that you submit a good quality cover letter is because the bosses need to see just how determined and interested you are in applying for the job. They want employees who can think out of the box, who are quick thinkers and who are very good in communication, and the best place to start would be how you communicate to the HR department. A cover letter template would make a great guide when making your own cover letter so check out some websites that cater to tips and articles on careers.

Mark Mattey is a writer and entrepreneur. To learn more about cover letter templates <http://www.coverlettersthatkill.com> or writing from a cover letter template <http://www.coverlettersthatkill.com> , visit his website.

Resume Writing Services May Be Your Only Chance of Getting Noticed

There is no doubt how stiff the competition is when it comes to getting hired especially these days when even the most qualified person is getting laid off.

What can get you hired?

The only way by which you can get noticed, which is your first goal when applying for a job, is to have a great looking resume. A great looking resume is not a resume that is printed on colored paper. A great looking resume is one that speaks how qualified you are to the position that you are vying for. It will be able to tell the recruiters that you are what they are looking for. It is not only about listing down the experiences that you had in the past years. It takes more than that.

That is why there is a growing number of people getting Resume Writing Services. You would be surprised that even the most experienced person when it comes to work experience gets these services. Let us face it, we all have our strengths and weaknesses and it is so hard to put our strengths on paper. If we do not know what we are doing, we might actually be putting the wrong information on our resume. Getting services for resume writing prevents you from doing that. After all, your resume is technically the company's first impression of you.

All it takes is a few seconds for a Human Resource personnel involved in the hiring process to scan your resume and put it in the reject pile or the "possible hires" pile. Thus, have a great looking resume ready, at all all times, even if you have to get resume writing services to have that.

Cheryl Forbes owns and operates the website http://www.cvbuddy.com

Free CV Help

As a professional recruiter and owner of a CV/resume writing business, I regularly come across great candidates all the time who wish they had asked or sought CV Help with their CV/resume before they submitted it to all those important jobs.

However, none of them think this help is free - how wrong could they be! They normally only learn this lesson once they have been rejected, and actually how much information and help is available to them for free.

The Statistics:

The statistics of the job search process are brutal. Most applicants learn form their mistakes, because getting to grips with the HR processes is too complex. But simple statistics can tell you much. In an average profile of applications to a typical job advert, whether that be via newsprint or the internet, the answers are:

- 20% of applicants are rejected because they don't include a Cover Letter
- 20% are rejected because they don't have the basic skills required
- 20% are rejected because of errors in their application - mostly spelling, also grammar

That last one is just a crazy statistic, and its one I always question when most good word processing programs include a spelling and grammar checker. But every month, my companies own statistics tell the same story!

So, how can candidates improve their chances of getting an interview

Free CV Help:

There are plenty of free resources to ensure that your CV is better presented:

- Microsoft: a majority of applicants will use MSWord to prepare their CV. So why not use the spell check, and the grammar check tools?
- Hewlett Packard: it is more difficult to see typing and grammatical errors in your CV on your PC screen. Once you are happy with a version of your CV, print it out
- A red pen: to ensure that the printed version is correct in both spelling (spell checkers ensure the words exist in English, not that they are the right words), and grammatically, scan it through using a red pen to lead your eye across the page. Mark any errors
- A highlighter pen: with a paper version of the job advert, use a highlighter to pick out the first five key skills/competencies. Now see if you can find the same five skills/competencies in your own CV. If you can't, you will be rejected
- Read it out loud: check that it reads well. To ensure this, stand up and read it out loud - this makes it easier to spot poor sentences
- Your eyes: Having printed out a now literally correct version of your CV, take each page and hold it out at arms length. Does it look correct, is there a balance between the black ink and white paper?

Now you have a version of your CV which probably contains at least ten less mistakes, and hence ten less reasons for rejection. However, this is only your own check, so there are two more free resources you can use before sending your CV in for a job application. Ideally, you need to use these resources at least three times to ensure the best optimised CV version.

Firstly, many Professional CV writers provide free CV/resume reviews. These are often - like our own - are marketing driven services, but offer dedicated self-CV writers excellent and ree access to professional resources. Secondly, there are also your riends. Ideally at least one could be a present or ex-HR profesional, but make sure it is read by at least one man, and one voman - women are generally more detail orientated, but you ever know who will be the first person to review your CV in the esired employer.

If candidates used this information and process to check heir CV's and ensure they were optimised for free, they would ignificantly reduce their chances of rejection, and increase their ossibility of interview.

Good Luck!

Ian R McAllister is the founder of Ajiri, a UK group focused ecruitment and employment in skills-short professional sectors, resently covering IT, telecoms and project management. Ajiri lso provides professional candidate information and services via series of online resources, including The Professional CV http://cv4.biz/> from CV4.biz and How To Write A Cover Letter http://www.howtowriteacoverletter.info/>

Divorced - Reentering the Job Market

Your divorce is final; you're back on the job market; the conomy sucks; now what? Take a deep breath -it will all be OK, I promise. Right now, you may not recognize yourself. Was there a car bomb?

No, it just feels that way. It must have been a powerful explosion because suddenly your old friends don't come around much and when they do, it's awkward. Your kids have also been affected by the blast--they're needier than ever and money is tight. Now as the dust settles, it's time to start digging through the rubble of what used to be your life.

My clients are a diverse group of people with backgrounds in the medical, military, educational, executive, or IT fields. As a professional resume writer who offers career coaching, cover letters, interview preparation, resumes packages, and complete job searches, I always stress to my clients: A resume's only purpose is to get you a job interview.

You're going to have to be especially courageous and resourceful to build your new life when there's so little left of your old one to build on. Although the rebuilding process seems overwhelming, it's not really when you break it down into baby steps. This baby step process is a systematic approach that will work in every corner of your life that you need to reconstruct. In this article, we're going to focus on getting back on your career feet.

Answer the following questions in writing and in detail. I realize this baby step may not feel like such a baby step but just do your best. There's a very empowering and practical reason for completing this questionnaire.

1. Name, address, and all contact information.
2. Are you looking for a new job with a new employer or a new job with your old employer?
3. What specific job are you seeking?
4. Are you switching jobs or re-entering the workforce?
5. Has your career followed a steady path or have there been detours?
6. Were these detours involved with being fired, jail, or career changes?
7. What previous jobs have you held?

8. Which is your stronger point-your skills or accomplishments?

9. Are you willing to relocate?

10. Describe your different jobs: dates, task performed, and how these tasks could affect the current job you're seeking.

11. For each task or accomplishment, describe it with an action verb such as managed, developed, authored, negotiated, or conceptualized.

12. For each task or accomplishment listed, how did it contribute to your company or department's bottom line? Use specific numbers and/or percentages if possible.

13. What is the highest level of education you completed? List schools, diplomas, majors, degrees, or certificates awarded.

14. List any academic awards or honors you received.

15. Describe your non-work experience: clubs, organizations, volunteer work?

16. List any special skills or hobbies which might have a direct bearing on the specific job you're looking for (languages, artistic ability, computers).

17. Have you ever been published? List the titles, subject matter, and where they were published.

18. Why are you the right person for this job? (Just the facts, ma'am.)

19. What really sets you apart over all the other applicants?

While the dust and smoke of divorce are clearing, it's easy to overlook all the good things you have to offer your new employer and, more importantly, to offer yourself. Use these answers as a reminder of what you are. You will see daylight again.

Brenda Lovelady

Five Tips For Writing Great Cover Letters

Job seekers often have questions about cover letters. They want to know if cover letters are necessary and if they help people get jobs. The answer is yes in both cases. Unless you are applying online using a resume builder, and the online application does not allow you to attach a cover letter, it is assumed that you will send a cover letter with every resume that you send out. Even if the ad simply says, "Send resume," make sure that you send a cover letter as well.

Here are some tips to make sure that your cover letter is effective:

Keep the cover letter brief. Three to four paragraphs are sufficient to make your point.

Tailor each cover letter to the specific position that you are applying to. Form letters will not catch a recruiter/hiring manager's eye. Be sure to highlight the qualifications that you possess that are mentioned in the ad that you are responding to. You want to emphasize to the reader that you are a good match for the job.

Try to find the name of the person who will be receiving the resume if at all possible. Recruiters/hiring managers will pay more attention if they are being addressed personally.

If you do not possess a qualification that is listed in the ad, don't mention it in your cover letter. There is no need to draw attention to any deficits. Generally speaking, hiring managers put out a wish list of qualifications. Those who come closest to meeting all of the qualifications are usually the ones called in for the interview.

Let the reader know exactly which ad you are responding to. Oftentimes large employers have several ads running at one time. To make it easier for the reader, mention where you saw the ad, and if there is a reference number, be sure to include it in the cover letter.

Cheryl Palmer, M.Ed. is a career coach and a certified professional resume writer. She is the founder of Call to Career, a career coaching firm that assists people in finding their niche or calling in life.

Combining her professional status as a career coach with her love of writing, Ms. Palmer has written articles such as Thank God It's Monday! which was published in Message magazine and Â?Finding a Job That Fits You Like a Glove which was published in Community Jobs. Both articles were well received and have given her additional visibility in her field.

Cheryl Palmer has also been a guest on a radio show entitled Insight on Coaching hosted by Tom Floyd where she discussed the needs of Generation X in the workplace and how managers from other generations can get the best out of this segment of the workforce.

In an article on HotJobs' website entitled The Art of Being Assertive, Ms. Palmer was quoted as a subject matter expert on how assertiveness can help a person advance in his or her career.

Easy-to-Follow Techniques For Cover Letter Writing

Are you clueless about cover letter writing? Well you definitely need not be, especially with the help of these easy-to-follow techniques for cover letter writing. So how do you get started on writing your cover letter? First things first, you should be knowledgeable about the company and the position that you are aiming for. An interviewer will certainly not like it if you are totally clueless about what kind of company they are and if you seem to not know the requirements for the position.

So before you start on your cover letter writing, what you need to do is to conduct a bit of research to give you a good edge over the others who will be applying for the same position. To further help you out in writing your cover letter, here are some simple techniques for cover letter writing that you need to keep in mind:

? Follow the business-style of writing a letter, keep things formal but not boring or stiff. That's a common mistake of a lot of people, because they try to hard to sound business-like, they usually end up sounding boring, and that is something that does not sit too well with interviewers.

? Do not forget to spell check your letter and proofread your grammar as well. Even if you are not applying to be a writer, it is still imperative that you do not sound like you a child still trying to learn the basics of writing in English. Read your letter, once, twice - even thrice if that's what it takes to get things right before you send it out to your prospective employers.

Mark Mattey is a writer and entrepreneur. To learn more about cover letter writing <http://www.coverlettersthatkill.com> or cover letter writing tips <http://www.coverlettersthatkill.com> , visit his website.

Ways to Write a Resume

How to write a resume - this is one big question that most pplicants are faced with. As scary as the question may sound, this s actually easy if you just gear yourself with the right information hat you need. First of all, you need to take note about your work xperience. Include those unpaid works and part time since they an create a good impression on your resume. Next, take note bout your education and job title that you have acquired through ime.

Note some of your job accomplishments, specially those najor ones. You can also list you membership on certain organiza-ions, special accomplishments, and military service if there is any. 'rom your list of skills, look for those that are transferable or hose skills that are somehow relevant to the job opening that you re applying for.

Start your resume writing by putting on your full name, ad-ress, fax, telephone number, and email. Create a good objective hat should be made in short sentences that describe the kind of vork that you wish to obtain. After then, write down your work xperience with your recent job. Don't forget to include the name f the company and the responsibilities that you hold in your job.

Always focus on your skills that you think is helpful for the ew company that you are applying on. You can also include elevant information about you like computer programming nowledge, languages spoken, etc. under the heading. Then you an follow other vital information about yourself. You can look for esume examples over the internet so you will be guided well.

Learn how to stand out from the crowd of job seekers <http://www.amazing-cover-letters.com/> and attract the attention of Hiring Manager.

Guidelines to Get That Job - Examples of Cover Letters

Before the challenges of carrying out the job duties comes the difficult task of sending out applications. To help out in composing your own, reading through examples of cover letters can let you in on the "what to do" and "what not to do" tips before letting your resume come under the scrutiny of an employer. Before you get to excited to cram up all your life's achievement in the letter, it is best to first analyze what you want the employer to know about you. A novel would definitely bore whoever the letter will be addressed to, not to mention that irrelevant details are not necessary and would not contribute to making your application stand out. One page is the recommended length of a cover letter - so as the saying goes, keep it short and sweet.

Remember that a fact of life is that the employers will hire you to get the job done - in short, you are to fulfill the company's needs and not the other way around. Do not include in your application, as you would notice in expertly written examples of cover letters, why you need the job desperately or how it would significantly help you in answering your financial problems. Be objective, formal and sincere. Keep the ideas of your letter coherent and clear. Each sentence should complement the previous to get an overall effect of inviting the audience to review your resume. Also be alert in checking spellings, punctuations and grammar, and once you've kept tab on these reminders, you are a step closer to bagging that dream job.

Mark Mattey is a writer and entrepreneur. To learn more about examples of cover letters <http://www.coverlettersthatkill.com> or cover letter examples and samples <http://www.coverlettersthatkill.com> , visit his website.

Your Quick and Simple Guide to Cover Letter Writing

Do you need to write a cover letter now - and fast? Well you certainly need not panic over something like this. Cover letter writing is not a daunting task that not everyone can do. As long as you keep an open mind about it, surely you will be able to easily come up with cover letters as fast as you need them. Are you now ready to get started on cover letter writing? Read on get some quick and simple steps.

? Keep things formal yet never ever boring: when it comes to writing anything, especially cover letters you should always be able to keep the attention of the person who is reading what you wrote. So why make a boring letter, right? Especially when it comes to cover letters, you should always be able to keep the reader's attention given that you he or she should remain interested enough for him or her to want to continue on reading up to the next part of your application.

? Don't forget to include the main point of your letter which is to talk about how much of a good fit you are to the company and to the position that you are applying for. The one thing that you should never ever forget about cover letter writing is that you should be able to point out all your best assets, especially for the job you are applying for. Make your cover letter sound like you will prove to be an asset to the company but do not sound boastful either.

Use those tips and you should be well on your way to creating a quality cover letter.

Mark Mattey is a writer and entrepreneur. To learn more about cover letter writing <http://www.coverlettersthatkill.com> or cover letter writing techniques <http://www.coverlettersthatkill.com> , visit his website.

Important Details to Learn From Sample Resume Cover Letters

Every application is valued through the element of a good impression and the capacity to make it better than most submitted ones. Since each day, a recruiting company would receive thousands of letters from hopefuls even with just one vacancy available; the challenge would then lie on how you can make your competitors seem more insignificant than yours. Sample resume cover letters are one of the ways in which you can gather tips and valuable advices to apply to your own, recognizing the fact that in the case of job hunting, first impressions certainly lasts.

The resume itself would be the so-called main course. But, even before the employer would proceed in analyzing the details about your experiences and achievements, you would have to set the mood first and make them interested. Be sure to do so without sounding redundant. Sample resume cover letters would teach you that in making your words complement your resume; the former would state the overall capacity for every job function and how it relates to the position you are applying for while the latter specifically details the achievements objectively.

Your cover letter is your opportunity to sell yourself, with the information contained on your resume backing up your claims on how effective you are for the job. Getting the employer nod their heads while reviewing what you have written would just about launch a good career for you and pave your way up the professional ladder. Inexperienced as some applicants may be, how good a written cover letter is would signify the potentialities of the candidate in while growing with that job.

Mark Mattey is a writer and entrepreneur. To learn more about sample resume cover letters <http://www.coverlettersthatkill.com> or sample cover letters and resumes <http://www.coverlettersthatkill.com> , visit his website.

Mining Resumes Advice and Tips

1. Make sure that the first page of your mining resume will quickly catch the employer's eye. A potential employer will spend 2 1/2 to 20 seconds on your mining resume.

2. Have a small introduction of yourself on the first page of your mining resume with what role you are seeking and what your goals are in the mining industry and have it linked to your cover letter which will be in more depth.

3. Font size should be no smaller than 11 point and should be a consistent size throughout the mining resume. The mining resume needs to be easy to read and text should be spread out evenly though out the resume. Use the same size and type of font for each heading used. Sounds easy but surprising how many people do not do this.

4. Remember that this is the first impression that make with your potential employer, so make it a good one. Consider taking up a professional mining resume service if you feel you will not give justice to yourself in writing your own mining resume.

5. Font type should be consistent throughout your mining resume

6. Try to keep the information in your mining resume relevant for the mining position you are applying for.

7. Make sure the referees know that you are using them, so when someone rings the referee they know straight away who you are and haven't forgotten you. It pays to ring them in advance to tell them that you are using them and that you are applying for mining employment, so they may get some phone calls over the next week. Plus a good way to catch up on your mining contacts/friends. Aim to have at least 2 and maximum of four. Also include how you know the person and state whether it's professional or a friend referee.

8. Birth date is optional in mining resumes.

9. Keep the mining resume positive and honest as you will •e found out later on if you enhance your resume too much.

10. You only need to put down the last three or relevant jobs ou have had.

11. List the duties involved in each job, the responsibilities nd the machinery and tools used.

12. List the licenses you have like your driver's license and ickets and qualifications you have. For example Marcsta, MWHS ard, HR license, MR licence, dump truck course, boiler maker icket, Fork Lift Licence, Provision of Qld Mining Generic Induc- ion (surface Coal & Metalliferous), Senior First Aid. List the dates hat these expire as this will show you are work ready.

13. You only need to put down the qualifications and work xperience that is relevant for a position. For example if you are vanting a cleaner position in a mining camp, it pays to show that ou have experience in this field, so list previous jobs that have imilar duties. If you are after a unskilled mining job it pays to nclude previous work history that shows the similar characteris- ics as the mining job requires.

14. With your qualifications and tickets state where you ob- ained them, Port Hedland, Kalgoorlie or Perth for instance and nclude the state in which you were trained for example Queen- land or Western Australia or North Territory. Also state how long he qualification took to obtain.

15. Identify keywords that mining companies look for in heir new employers; this can be done by reading mining job dvertisements that you are interested in and then make sure you re stating them with examples of your experience related to them n your resume and cover letter.

16. Keep your resume to the maximum three pages if not two. Mining companies what to quickly check that your suitable for the role with the correct experience and skills and the interview will enable you to explain parts of yourself in more detail.

17. Check that your email is a good for potential future employers to read. Too many times people have a email address like (angryman(at)hotmail.com, which gives the potential employer a chance to stereotype which can affect your chance.

18. Personalise your introduction statement. Too many times people use an introducing statements which looks like it come straight of the internet. Write in first person, so it should start off with for example using (" I am" a competent worker) not in second person like ("A" competent worker)

19. Successful resumes used for obtaining employment in the mines are different than resumes that you would use for jobs back in the city. Using a resume format and structure that is not normal for the mining industry is going to cause you delays in obtaining mining employment.

20. Its pays to get a second opinion from a friend or from a professional resume service provider that your resume gives you justice and is suitable for the mining industry and that there isn't silly spelling mistakes that you haven't picked up yet.

21. If you are living in New Zealand or and out of the state and applying for a mining job in Western Australia for example. Include your area code and the international code for New Zealanders in your resume contact details. (+64 international code for NZ)

Too many people that we come across are failing to obtain a mining job in Western Australia, places like Kalgoorlie, Port Hedland, Leinster, Raventhorpe, Tom Price, Karratha, and in Queensland in area like Emerald and Mount Isa.

Simply because they have tried to save money by doing the resume writing themselves which in the end has cost them lot more as they are missing out on high paying mining jobs before taking up our service.

If this is the first time entering the mining industry and not having any success to date. Feel welcome to send your resume to the only professional mining resume service, our email address is below and we will give you a honest opinion of your resume and tell you whether its fit for the mining industry and its totally free. When you send in your resume to the email address below please include what types of mining jobs you are interested in the mines.

We have the expertise to do very provide you with a professional resume for labouring, industrial, mining, farming, oil, factory jobs. Satisfaction Guaranteed.

For a free assessment of your resume send it to resumeservice@getajobinthemines.com

Or for more information about our professional mining resume service <http://www.getajobinthemines.com/mining-resume.html> go here to visit http://www.getajobinthemines.com/mining-resume.html

Why Do You Need to Browse Through Sample Resume Cover Letters?

The answer is simple, but the importance of the time taken in browsing through sample resume cover letters is often neglected by job applicants. Professionals from different fields have offered advice to aspiring hunters on what employers generally expect from their applicants, that when added with the personal flavor or the unique impressive written style of an individual, makes him or her rise above other applicants. Getting aware of what are considered plus and minus points are highly effective. True enough, confidence is a crucial factor that employers look out for in their applicants, but it is already a different matter when the confidence is pointless and directionless.

Relying on your own skills in writing a cover letter is an important facet. However, so is being resourceful and open-minded in searching for ways to improve yourself, which in this case, is your job application. There are a lot of sample resume cover letters that, though you are not encouraged to copy them verbatim, will help you in developing your own by consolidating the ideas from different point of views and eventually allowing you to have a final output which is yours. So, once you have your eye on that dream job, the first thing is to formulate an effective and impressive way of getting your application noticed - the good way, and not because you would have committed every violation possible. So, on a final note, the acceptance in a job relies on your credentials and qualifications, and a cover letter is one of the first steps in manifesting that.

Mark Mattey is a writer and entrepreneur. To learn more about sample resume cover letters <http://www.coverlettersthatkill.com> or cover letter samples and examples <http://www.coverlettersthatkill.com> , visit his website.

The Basics Behind the Right Cover Letter Format

Are you interested to find out the secret behind getting that dream job of yours? While you certainly need to do good in your interview and have good credentials, if not stellar credentials, the other thing that you should not take for granted when you are applying for a job is your cover letter. For those who are quite clueless on what a cover letter is - especially since a lot of people do not ever bother to make one when they are giving out their job or internship applications, this is what you should know about the basics behind the right cover letter format.

A cover letter will serve as an introduction about yourself, a way for you to give the interviewer a background on who you are, your objectives for applying, and your interests. As interviewers do not really have the luxury of time when it comes to talking to applicants, a letter that is written in the right cover letter format will be able to cover all the basics that the interviewers need to see if you have the right stuff for their company.

So what are the basics that you need to know for the right cover letter format? Firstly, make it clear and concise. No interviewer will be pleased to see a cover letter that is more than a page long. Remember, they do not have the luxury of time to go through your whole family history nor do they actually want to find out about it. What is important is that you are able to talk about your interest in the job and that you are able to show your sincerity in working for the company. However, do not ever sound like you are sucking up to them, just be genuine, and if you really are sincere then it will definitely shine through your cover letter.

Mark Mattey is a writer and entrepreneur. To learn more about correct cover letter format <http://www.coverlettersthatkill.com> or cover letter writing tips <http://www.coverlettersthatkill.com> , visit his website.

Writing a Wining CV Profile

How you write and present your CV profile is the golden key to capturing and holding your readers attention. Employers and recruiters are sometimes flooded by job applications and working through loads of CVs can be a tedious task. However it is possible to present you Curriculum Vitae a way which will set it apart from the rest.

Apart from your CV's profile you'll need to focus attention on the style, layout, headings and most of all on the content.

To make your Curriculum Vitae or resume stand out from the rest it will be in your interest to make sure you include the following headings:

Cover Letter / Profile
Work Experience
Career achievements
Qualifications
Goals
References

Apart from the headings it is quite important to focus on their order as well. In the majority of cases employers prefer to receive CVs in the same layout. This makes their job a lot easier. And if you can present your CV in a suitable way this will immediately merit your CV.

Start off with the CV Profile or CV Cover Letter. This should consist of a brief overview of your whole CV, however do not disclose too many details here. In this CV Profile you would like to aptivate your prospective employer's attention and make them ead your whole CV. How to do this is quite straight forward and ou do not have to be a writer to do this.

There is help out there and the CV Profile website offers all his data at no cost to jobseekers.

For more information on how to write a winning CV Cover etter and to receive a Free CV Profile Example, visit the CV 'rofile specialists.

For more information on how to write a winning CV Cover etter and to receive a Free CV Profile Example <http://cv-rofile.co.uk/cv-profile/cv-profile-example/> , visit the CV Profile http://cv-profile.co.uk/cv-profile/> specialists.

The Resume Service

A resume will serve as your gate pass for you to be able to and on the job that you are eying for. However, not all people are ifted with the ability of writing a responsive resume that will tand out among the rest hence there are resume service these ays.

What are the benefits of going for resume service? Well, one hing that you can get from their service is the ability to create a esume that will excel above others without actually putting ourself in a lot of stress of looking for the right words to merge ogether towards your benefit. Of course, their works would come with a price but if you try to think about the benefit that you will get from their service, you will see that the price is not really something to fret about.

In looking for someone who can write your resume for you, it is wise to give her a complete background about your accomplishments and backgrounds. You may want to speak out your weaknesses and strengths so the one who will write for you will be able to put these informations on your resume in the sense that your positive traits will overshadow your negative characters. If you wish to get the best out of their service, you should confirm first the reliability of such person so you would get the best out of their work. Of course since you are going to spare your cash, might as well get something that will make your spending worthy. Look around for someone who were given good reviews by other people who tried their service.

Learn how to stand out from the crowd of job seekers <http://www.amazing-cover-letters.com/> and attract the attention of Hiring Manager.

A Resume Format

If you are making your resume, the first question that would probably pop up into your head is-what resume format should I follow? Well, with so many to choose from, you will really have a hard time looking for the right one to use.

Truth is, you can make use of whatever you like as long as such resume format will exude the sense of professionalism. Avoid the use of too fancy fonts or those that are too small since this will sacrifice the readability of the resume. Try to shun away from too many additions like underlines, bold fonts, and even italicized letters since this will lessen the sense of expertise of your work. You should also prevent the use of too many kinds of fonts, as much as possible stick to only one.

Put in mind that employers would often detect your own personality depending upon the resume format that you use hence it is only right to look for the kind of format that will match your personality. If you think that one format is fitted on you then you should not feel skeptical in using it. Now, if you can't find any then you should not lose your patience in looking because before the day ends, you will surely find the one that will give you a sense of satisfaction and contentment.

Looking for resume format is easy now because of the availability of information over the internet. All you have to do is to make a simple visit and you can expect to find the answers to all of your questions.

Learn how to stand out from the crowd of job seekers <http://www.amazing-cover-letters.com/> and attract the attention of Hiring Manager.

Your Google CV

First Impressions Count!

Whether it is over the phone, face to face or online, the first contact anyone has with you will affect their opinion of you - for life.

Online, the main way to initially "meet people" is via search engines. Most people nowadays will conduct a quick search on someone they are about to hire, interview or network with. With personal online visibility playing such a large role in today's world, ensuring that you make a good first impression via the search engine result pages is essential. These listings have become known as your Google CV.

What is Your Google CV?

Online, your reputation is translated from what appears on the first three pages of the results that Google returns when your name is searched for. Very few searchers will progress beyond the first ten results of a search and it is vital that your most important information appears here. Just like a traditional CV, everyone needs to have a Google CV and it should feature the "you" that you want people to see.

Step One in the Google CV Process

The first thing to do is to make sure that you actually appear in the top listings of Google. You are unlikely to have a unique name - unless Frank Zappa is your father - so it is up to you to make sure that you are the Joe Smith who is number one. It may also be possible that other people have written some negative things about you. These should never be the first results that people find, meaning you need to add more content to push these negative mentions down the rankings and away from page one.

It is also not good enough for the first Google result to be about you purely because you were photographed at the latest club opening in your city. This will not impress most future employers or clients. The first few results on your Google CV need to portray you as how you want to be seen - a fundamental step on online self-marketing. If you are looking for a new job, your first few results need to be professional and informative or, if you are building your online blogging / website profile, a little more personal information and motivation to visit your site could be needed.

How to Build Your Google CV

This all sounds well and good, but many people are lost when it comes to making it happen. Thankfully, there are some easy things to remember when successfully building your Google CV:

Have a website - There are few better ways to control your persona online than by having your own website / blog.

? Create good content - If you have a website or blog, make sure that it is regularly updated with quality content to help make you the leading expert in your field.

? Become involved - Having a strong online presence by participating in areas like forums and commenting on blogs will increase the amount of cross-linking that occurs around your name.

? Network socially - Having an active profile on sites like LookupPage, Facebook and LinkedIn will help you make valuable connections. These sites also rank well on Google and offer trusted links to your website.

? Contribute online - This could be by commenting wherever you can (good, informative commentary of course) or in the form of articles. By becoming a regular contributor to the myriad of online article directory sites, you can come to be considered an expert in your field and fill the results pages with informative content, all courtesy of you.

? Sign up with a web presence builder - These online offerings, like LookupPage, can guide you through the process of building a comprehensive and successful Google CV

<http://www.lookuppage.com/lookup-page/about> - doing most of the hard work for you and acting as a pivotal component of your online self-marketing.

By allowing you to create or improve your online presence, Lookup Page <http://www.lookuppage.com> can help you to take control of your Google CV and start branding yourself online. LookupPage's advanced technology and products then allow you to protect your reputation through its focus on simplicity, track-ability and visibility.

How to Create a Professional Resume - Essential Resume Writing Tips That You Must Know

These days, if you want to get hired by an employer you need a professional looking resume. No longer can you simply get a job by sending in a resume you created within 2 minutes. You need to be head and shoulders above your competition. If you want that job, you need to learn how to create a professional resume. In this article I'm going to share with you some tips that you can use to create a professional resume.

Do you know the two biggest mistakes that job seekers make on their resume? They either provide too much information, or they provide too little. An employer doesn't have a lot of time to actually read resumes all the way through. If you provide too much nformation your resume won't get read. Period. If you don't rovide enough information, then it seems you aren't enthusiastic bout the company.

You need to find a middle ground. Short sentences are better. Employers skim read resumes. So it's better to use short entences. Tailor your resume to each job you applied for. Take ut information that is irrelevant. Use plenty of line breaks. And eplace boring words, with some exciting and bold words.

At the end of the day, it all comes down to the layout of your esume. The way it looks. Most job seekers out there have no idea ow to correctly format their resume. If you format your resume orrectly and get the layout right you'll be a head of the competion. You'll be able to get hired by any employer you want.

That's why I recommend you pick up some software that ill format your resume correctly and replace boring words with ower words that will excite a potential employer. Let your experince and qualifications get you through an interview, but let your rofessional looking resume dazzle the employer who will give you hat interview.

Go   here http://www.squidoo.com/amazingresumecreator>   to discover ow to create a professional resume with amazing resume creator http://www.squidoo.com/amazingresumecreator> !

2 'New' Cover Letters to Get You Hired!

Here's your chance to do what few other job hunters don't write two powerful cover letters that will put you in front of the pack. You might be wondering what this is all about. A cover letter's a cover letter, isn't it? Now am I telling you there are various flavors? That's exactly what I'm saying. With millions of people looking for jobs each year, you need to try something new. Forget vanilla letters. Let's go for rocky road and praline chip.

#1: Networking Cover Letter

The networking cover letter helps you reach out to the people in your life who can help you the most -- family members, friends, neighbors, associates, and professional men and women. They can assist you in making contacts you might never be able to make on your own. Ask them for employment leads, referrals from their circle of influence, advice, knowledge, and even personal introductions.

To achieve these leads, start with a master list of everyone you can think of. Take out those old business cards you stuffed in a pocket or drawer. Look at association rosters, church directories, e-mail address books, any and all groups you are affiliated with. Then send your networking cover letter to each person on the list, asking for help. This will take some time to accomplish but it will pay off, I promise you that. The more people who know about you and what you need and want, the greater the results.

Networking Cover Letter Tips:

* Limit your letter to one page.

* List your abilities and strengths.

* Ask for job leads and referrals.

* Clip your resume to the cover letter.

* Send a thank you note to those who respond.

#2: The All-In-One Resume Cover Letter

The resume cover letter combines the best of a cover letter and resume in one. This letter is an ideal tool to catch the interest of recruiters, headhunters, and agencies where brevity and speed are essential.

Condense the essentials from your resume and put them in a bulleted list within the letter itself. Strive for one page. This powerful document helps you gain attention, make your point, and ask for what you want.

So why wait another minute? Step up to the task of landing that dream job with these two letters that will increase your 'net' worth: the networking cover letter and an all-in-one resume cover letter.

Want even more free cover letter tips <http://www.coverlettercentral.com/jimmy-sweeney-cover-letters.htm> from Jimmy Sweeney? Get *loads* of free advice to help write great cover letters ... visit http://www.coverlettercentral.com/jimmy-sweeney-cover-letters.htm now.

Jimmy Sweeney is the president of CareerJimmy and author of several career related books and writes a monthly article titled, "Job Search Secrets."

Resume Writing - 5 Words You Should Never Use on Your Resume

Human Resources professionals are inundated with resumes on a daily basis. Now, more than ever before, job seekers must learn to make their resumes stand out. One of the simplest and more effective ways to do this is by using power words and phrases. These words add muscle to your resume statements and exhibit intelligence. Search online for resume power words and you will be overwhelmed by the amount of websites that claim to 'provide' the complete list of resume power words.

Some power word sites list several words as power words that are NOT power words at all. Your resume can land up in the reject pile if you use the wrong phraseology.

Five words you should never use on your resume are:

A lot - This is probably the most obvious in the list. The problem with saying 'a lot' is that the phrase is entirely too vague. 'A lot' probably means something different to you from what the phrase means to me. There is no value in the phrase 'a lot.' One girl saying, "I eat a lot of chocolate," could mean something entirely different from another girl making the same statement. How much is 'a lot?'

Instead of saying, "I did XYZ a lot of the time," you could say, "I did XYZ 16 hours per work week." The more specifications you add to your resume, the better your chances are of getting an interview.

Creative - Should someone who boasts of being creative actually have to come right out and say they are creative? Probably not. The best way to show creativity is by accentuating accomplishments or skills you have that emphasize your creativity.

Flexible - Flexible is so overused that the word has lost all power. Flexible does not impress anyone. Flex that muscle on top of your head and come up with another power word that gets the same idea across.

If you are applying for a job where physical flexibility is critical (i.e. ballerina or yoga master) feel free to leave this word on your resume.

Interesting - Interesting as a power word is not interesting enough to grab or keep the attention of a human resources executive. Using stronger power words will create the idea that you are interesting and companies will be interested in calling you for an interview. Anyone truly interesting will never come right out and say that they are!

It - Using 'it' in place of actually telling what 'it' means confuses most readers.

Want another reason to cut 'it' out?

You automatically appear more intelligent.

Using power words can boost the effectiveness of your resume.

For more words that should never appear on your resume, check out the free e-book "197 Words You Should Never Use on Your Resume <http://www.resumedictionary.com/words-that-should-not-be-on-your-resume/> " written by the creators of http://www.ResumeDictionary.com

Freelance writer and high school English teacher.

Top 3 Tips How to Format a Winning CV

1. MAKE USE OF ALL AVAILABLE SPACE AND FORMATTING

A good graduate Curriculum Vitae should not exceed 2 pages. Research proves that no more than 48% of interviewers read past page 1. In other words, if you CV is 2 pages make sure you have all the important stuff (e.g. what makes YOU stand out) in the first page and treat page 2 as more of an annex. If the recruiter does not read it, no big deal.

Having said this, you can put a LOT of information in one page. Use tables in word, they are an easy way of making good use of space while making sure that everything is aligned as it should be. It is impressive the number of CVs that have grey boxes, lines, double lines, etc. Always ask yourself: how do they help you stand out? They don't.

They only take precious recruiter attention away from the facts that make you a top candidate.

2. USE STANDARD FONTS AND COLOURS, PDF IF POSSIBLE

Arial or Times New Roman work best, white background with white text. No fancy animations. Many people (especially at interview stage) will print the CV on paper therefore any non-standard colours and animations will not come through and will make the CV look odd.

If you are sending your resume in electronic format try sending it in PDF format rather than MS Word if possible. It looks much more professional and you are guaranteed that the layout on the receiving end will be what you want it to be.

3. MAKE SURE THERE ARE NO TYPOS, SPELLING ERRORS, ETC

Any of those errors would get your CV straight into the trash a good 90% of the time. The interviewer would think: "If you didn't bother taking 2 minutes to spell check your CV before applying why should I hire you and spend months training you?"

C'mon, you have spell check tools everywhere - how on earth can you have a mistake on your resume?

Make sure all formatting is consistent. Example, if you say you studied in "Berlin, Germany" then you need to use the same [City], [Country] format anywhere else in the CV

CONCLUSION

Your CV is your business card. You have days, weeks, months to prepare it. You can ask for help either from friends, family or professionals. There is NO reason on earth why it should not be outstanding. The two primary reasons for rejection at entry-level positions (i.e. graduate level)

1.   Simple mistakes that prove lack of preparation and attention to detail
2.   Not having in mind what the recruiter wants to know and instead dumping dates and degrees and waiting for the interviewer to decipher them and work out why you are the best candidate.

Following these tips will get you a long long way into landing the job offer, with little effort.

Agustin Valecillos is a Vice President at a top tier Investment bank focussing on Commodities and FX Structuring. He is also the Founder and CEO of a team of Investment Banking professionals who pride themselves in helping people jump-start their investment banking career :http://www.helpmegetajob.co.uk> in the financial services sector through an outstanding banking CV, cover letter and appli-

cation form. For the latest techniques, visit
http://www.helpmegetajob.co.uk

Evaluating Your Resume Through Unbiased Eyes

Can you do it?

Can you step back, assume the role of a neutral and impartial observer, and accurately assess the fruits of your labor?

Unless you're a practiced editor, it's not easy.

To begin with, this is an important document; you've probably put a lot of time and effort into revising it. The resulting sense of ownership can be hard to disassociate from.

More importantly, when you review your resume you inevitably see a complete picture of the person described...because it's you. Missing pieces of data, any lack of clarity, points that aren't as strong as they could be - these are harder for you to discern because you have an exhaustive knowledge of the subject matter. Your brain has the information it needs to fill in the blanks automatically, so they may not register as such.

Even when it comes to seemingly more benign issues such as page layout, it can be a challenge to critique your work objectively (and whatever you do...don't underestimate the importance of layout and design).

As difficult as it may be, you've got to acquire the ability to critically review your resume. Either that, or you need to find someone whose judgment you trust to help you with this task.

Whether or not you have success at the early stages of the hiring process will, in large part, be determined by your ability to successfully execute this step.

There's a good chance the hiring manager who's preparing to pick up your resume does not know you. Therefore, his brain isn't going to fill in any blanks or clarify ambiguous information. He's got nothing to go on but the words you sent to him.

You'd better make sure you're telling a complete, comprehensible, compelling story. You've got to present the information in such a way that a quick scan catches his attention...and peaks his interest enough that he slows down and actually reads it.

Don't become so enamored of what you've written that you lose the ability to look at it through someone else's eyes. Someone who has never met you. Someone who may be sifting through hundreds of other resumes - all representing people vying for the same position.

Sometimes it's not easy to critically judge your own resume.

Remember, though - the hiring manager isn't going to have any such difficulty.

Rebecca Metschke helps professionals improve their marketability. The author of The Interview Edge (http://www.TheInterviewEdge.com), a comprehensive career guide to career management, she also writes a daily blog posting strategies, tips and advice for those whose careers are in transition.

http://blog.TheInterviewEdge.com

Resume Miseries - Are You Making Any of These 3 Deadly Mistakes With Your Resume?

It's not your fault . You don't write resumes for a living. I see many people blow it because college professors, friends, and neighbors give hearsay advice. It's confusing.

Let's look at 3 deadly resume writing mistakes and misunderstandings and move to what you should do instead.

Mistake #1 - Using Bill Gates' Word Resume Templates - Why not? It's easy. Fill in the blanks. Done. Stop. Ask what would happen if all applicants used Microsoft resume templates? What one word would recruiters, interviewers, and prospective employers think? My guess: "lazy."

What To Do Instead - Focus on prospective employer (reader). Find a real person resume you like. Does the result look professional and customized to a job opening? Is there plenty of white space? Are margins at least one inch wide all the way around text? Is type size bigger than 10pt; ideally 12pt? Is there an absence of ruled and underscore lines? From scratch adapt what you see to your needs. Read rest of this article to avoid two other deadly mistakes.

Mistake #2 - Failing to include results (accomplishments, achievements). Too often people bang out performed tasks (copied from job descriptions). They are Key Job Requirements (KJRs). Boring. Your resume is not alone. It will be one of hundreds seen by underpaid resume screeners, secretaries, and HR "analysts." Their job? Find reasons to NOT keep your resume.

What To Do Instead - Showing results under a tight one or two-line summary of the job's purpose causes the screener to spend more than the typical 11 seconds (not minutes) with your document. Don't bullet KJRs. Only bullet results. Train the reader: "Bullets mean achievements or accomplishments, not job tasks." Start with the result. Use numbers, dollars, and percents. Next, state action, e.g., how you achieved the result? Short. Brief.

Mistake #3 - Listing three, four or more juicy references - Wrong, not right! Cart before the horse. Your top purpose is to get a phone or in-person interview. You have rights. How do you know you will want to work there? If the organization is interested, you will supply list of references. Please don't say, "References on request." That's hokey. Not cool.

What To Do Instead - Wait. Wait until the employer rep asks for references. Then match each reference to person contacting your references. VPs want to talk to VPs. HR wants to talk to HR people. Director level to director level. Crucial. Include title and your relationship with each reference. Supervisor? Owner? Champion? These are work references, not ministers, pals, or family members.

And now I would like to invite you to claim your Free Access to sample professional two-page resumes, resume templates, biographical sketches, and other search tools to help you land your new job faster. Visit http://www.resumesteve.com/ and take part in a confidential, Free, live, and interactive job search, resume and cover letter critique teleseminar Sundays at 9PM US EST. Thank you for reading this entire article.

Stephen Q Shannon The Free Teleseminar Resume Guy!

Resume 101 - Proofreading Your Resume - Sink Or Swim?

Proofreading is a specialized skill and MS Word only gets about one third of the job done. So if you were relying on the spell check feature to finish your proofreading don't even dream of using that resume just yet. Most resume services offer editing and proofreading as part of their services. So you don't have to go it all alone. One simple email will usually do the trick. Realistically your resume should be perfect as it represents you to a potential employer. But the least I can do is give you some helpful shortcuts here. Should you wish to go it on your own here is a list of common pitfalls you will want to check for:

? First take your time. Remember to set it aside for a while and give it an objective look a day later when you are more detached. Start by reading it aloud slowly word by word and see if it all makes sense. While you are doing this ask yourself is this what my employer would want to see?

? On your second review read out loud, you will look for spelling errors and punctuation errors. You may find it easier to read from the bottom up for this as you can slowly isolate each word.

? Is the format visually attractive? Could it be improved? I lways recommend printing your documents before beginning roofreading. The flat no glare nature of paper allows all the errors o be seen. This is twice as effective as using the computer screen y the way.

? A tip that works is to have a skilled proof reading partner, r use a ruler to only read one line of text at a time. Slower is etter, as two gaffs that slip through could lead to rejection.

? Make sure your punctuation and spacing is consistent hroughout by scanning at arms length.

? Check for common trouble spots like Homonyms, there & heir for example, spelling of all proper names, wrong words like sing: or rather than of, brain rather than Brian as this will be lways missed by the spell checker.

? Check for missing letters that still makes a word and other ypos. When you need your and the r is left off the end it still nakes a correctly spelled word, but it doesn't work in the sen- ence.

? Check for errors in logic. Critical, make sure you focus on- y on the meaning of what you read.

? Omissions are one of the most common errors. The writer ill often miss these as they know what they meant of course. Ience the importance of a proof reading service or at least an diting partner.

? Numerical typos in addresses, phone numbers, emails, nd dates again the spell checker will not help. You must individu- lly verify each and every one of these.

? Grammar check: If you visit or call your grammar seek rofessional writing and proofreading help as your resume and over letter are your sole representation in securing an employ- nent interview.

? The Gregg Reference Manual or The Associated Press Stylebook are must read reference manuals.

But if you are not already familiar with them it would be best to seek professional help. Most folks are not aware that proofreading services are affordable. It is not something you can do in a hurry.

? Beware of the MS Word program's tendency to make the first letter in every line capitalized if the auto-correct option is on.

? To avoid common cut and paste problems make sure you use only the space bar and arrow keys to format your text the way you want. The purpose of a cut and paste box for a resume and a cover letter is to destroy all formatting (MS Word smart quotes, Tabs, Text boxes, multiple columns etc. are lost.)

Carefully consider the penalty for a faulty or mediocre resume and cover letter in your job search. Please know and understand all the best writers routinely use editors and proofreaders. It is not really that difficult to get help if you need it. Consider for example a recent search of the term: Resume Writers returned more than 43,000,000 results from Google. I often recommend the study of a popular book on proofreading, even if you possess great writing ability already. As this free info article is only designed to be helpful in pointing the way. College courses in proofreading have several prerequisites so don't dive into shallow water from a tall cliff. The whole goal is to make your resume as polished and professional as possible.

(c) 2009 Darrell Z. DiZoglio of http://RighteousResumes.com The website for free job hunting assistance and strategies. Publishers may reprint this entire article if my links are included. "PAY IT FORWARD." Use my free resume review service, free resume samples, Cover letter samples, expert advice & free info articles. For recession busting specials on all the professional services you need go here: http://www.RighteousResumes.com/services.html

Would you like to find out how the competition got the job you wanted? (Visit on the above link.)

You do know your resume and cover letter is the sink or swim, mission critical part of your job hunt right?

Simple Resume Tip

Once you've finished your resume, don't send it out until you have someone else look at it. Even if its just your spouse, a second pair of eyes can always see mistakes, or omissions, in a piece of work, and it's better to find mistakes before the resume is sent out for the first time.

That's a simple resume tip, but it's an important one.

Other resume tips to consider are:

1. Put your resume on the web. There are plenty of job search sites on the web, like Monster.com - which is a general site, or specific sites dedicated to certain industries - for example AvJob that lists aviation jobs, and so on. Use a PDF rather than a scanned version of your resume, it looks nicer and is more professional.

2. Update your resume on a regular basis. It used to be that many people would get one job and work their way up through a single company, but the business atmosphere is much different now. Chances are people will move from job to job. Therefore,

update your resume at least once a month, with any new achievements you've accomplished, any new organizations you've joined, or any new certifications. Don't put it off and put it off until finally five years have passed, and all of a sudden you need to update that resume and you can't remember half of what you've achieved in that time.

3. There are certain professions for which certifications have to be passed on a six-month or annual basis. Academics have to publish regularly or basis or perish. One should always grow in one's job - if not for advancement than at least for job satisfaction!

4. If you're not getting the response from your resume that you expected -- if you're sending out dozens of resumes and getting only one or two responses - have a professional business coach look at your resume and see if it needs improvement and in what areas.

Don't know the first thing about creating a resume <http://www.employmentblawg.com/2009/creating-a-resume> ? Gary Lawson can help! Gary did his fair share of pavement pounding before he realized the key to successful job hunting is in the RESUME. Today, he writes career-related articles for popular blog EmploymentBlawg.Com <http://www.employmentblawg.com/> . Check out Gary's resumé series when you visit the site today!

Resume Format Sample - Tips, Tips, and More Tips

Putting together a resume is not quite as difficult as putting together a book, but it does take a certain amount of skill to make sure it looks as professional as possible and conveys the proper impression to your potential employers.

There's no need to sit at your computer and try to decide how to put together this resume. Take a look at a resume format sample. You can find hundreds of these samples on the web. These samples are available for a variety of professions.

Executive resumes - those used for people looking for six-figure jobs in the management fields, will convey more and different kinds of information than professional resumes - those resumes for people in the white and blue-collar fields who actually do the work! Professional resumes are for people like accountants, construction consultants, salespeople, nurses and so on.

Public sector resumes - those used by military people who have separated from the military and are now looking for jobs in government. People who work for politicians are also considered part of the public sector. Then there are student resumes - the students aren't necessarily looking for jobs but rather for entrance into a certain institution of higher learning.

You can never look at too many resume format sample(s).

Obviously you are not going to borrow some of the job entries and experience listed on those samples (some people have been so desperate that they've actually tried this. Rest assured, prevaricating on resumes will be found out, especially in today's climate.) However, it's helpful just to see the way the resumes are formatted and the types of information that are included.

You will find these sites very helpful as you pursue your goal of a new job, or a better one that that which you now have.

Feeling torn over what to use for your resume style <http://www.employmentblawg.com/2009/resume-style</a> ? Gary Lawson can help! Gary did his fair share of pavement pounding before he realized the key to successful job hunting is in the

RESUME. Today, he writes career-related articles for popular blog EmploymentBlawg.Com <http://www.employmentblawg.com/> . Check out Gary's resumé series when you visit the site today!

5 Insider Tips You Must Know For Writing Your Executive Resume

If you're an executive searching for your next opportunity in today's hotly competitive market, you've probably found that the task of marketing yourself is unlike any other.

How do you sum up a long, storied career in just a few paragraphs? What is the best way to differentiate yourself on paper--and to get others to focus on this value?

Standing out among the pack requires an intense emphasis on your natural leadership abilities, the impact you have on your employer's businesses, the feedback you get from colleagues, and the hard skills that you bring to the table.

This information comprises what is known as a "personal brand," and it has become the cornerstone of a successful executive resume in the employment arena.

Here are 5 insider tips that can help bring out your personal brand--and get your resume to open more doors for you:

1 - Hone Your Message.

Many executive resumes contain too much detail, which is quite understandable given the long tenure that many candidates possess.

However, it's asking a lot of hiring authorities to wade through more than 2 or 3 pages of information.

My recommendation? Sharpen the intensity of your branding message by zeroing in on your top 3-5 main qualifiers, including success stories and keywords that back these up.

In addition, focus on one career goal and skill set at a time. This may mean that you will create one resume targeting a role as COO, and another that describes your skills for a VP of Sales position.

2 - Don't Bury the Lead.

As we used to say in journalism, get your critical information all up front and ready for the reader to absorb.

Just started a high-level MBA program? Get it on the front page. Held roles of increasing scope that lead to your destination as CEO? Make it obvious.

Don't bury this type of key information on page 2 of your resume. The top half of the first page is prime "resume real estate," and your main qualifications deserve center stage here.

In addition, many executives benefit from a branding statement, which is a short sentence that serves as a marketing tagline. You can develop this sentence by jotting down some ideas on what you bring to the table, and how you achieve it.

A great branding tagline will tap into the heart of what you offer, such as these examples culled from the front-page position on executive resumes:

"COO Who Leverages Business Competencies to Create Profitable Ventures with Exceptional ROI"

"Strategic & Operational Leader for Real Estate Investment/Master Planning"

3 - Tell Your Story.

Most executives are able to spout figures and facts about their achievements, but it's the story behind these accomplishments that will add weight to the resume.

Consider looking at your results in light of the C-A-R (Challenge-Action-Result) strategy, which asks you to describe the situation you faced at work (Challenge), what you did when faced with it (Action), and of course, the outcome (Result) that occurred.

The C-A-R formula is popular for a reason--these anecdotes can also form the basis for success stories that you can also use as a basis for your next executive interview.

4 - Carefully Format Your Presentation.

When creating an executive resume, it's important to differentiate yourself from both your direct competition, plus distinguish yourself from lower-level applicants--and this means that it is best to make your document DIFFERENT from all the others.

Searching the Internet for executive resume samples will show you that there are many choices for font, format, and graphics that give flair to an executive resume presentation.

Above all, refrain from using the classic Microsoft Word template for your resume. Doing so will make your qualifications blend in rather than stand out, and lay the foundation for lackluster results.

5 - Use Those Glowing References.

Got testimonials? If so, you're in good shape, as these form a key part of a successful personal brand.

Better yet, including this information on your executive resume will allow you to back up the stories you've told about your achievements.

Many executives are able to use a quote or letter of reference as a striking addition to their leadership resume, especially when it reflects what they've already noted about their skills and competencies.

If you don't have access to this information, be sure to seek out colleagues, supervisors, customers, and even suppliers as a source of positive feedback. Then, take a shorter version of the most powerful testimonial to use as an endorsement.

As an example, a COO targeting a lateral move might be able to include a quote such as "Ted's resourcefulness and ingenuity are without equal. I have witnessed his ability to grow a startup into a maturing business and develop a multimillion-dollar venture in a difficult economic environment," from a corporate officer onto the executive resume--thereby verifying performance from a key reference source.

In summary, there are many ways to develop a masterpiece executive resume. It's important to ensure that hiring authorities can quickly cut to the heart of your qualifications--and consider you for prime opportunities that closely match your talents.

Laura   Smith-Proulx <http://www.anexpertresume.com/about.htm> , CCMC, CPRW, CIC is a credentialed, certified Executive Resume Writer and former recruiter with a 98% success rate opening doors to prestigious jobs through the use of personal branding techniques. The Executive   Director   of   An   Expert   Resume <http://www.anexpertresume.com> , her work has received international recognition as a global award nominee and contributor to career bestsellers.

Waitress Resume - Writing the Resume That Gets That Job

A professional waitress resume is a must if you are planning on working at an up market restaurant because chances are they are going to be expecting a good professional waitress resume from you. Gone are the days where restaurants were unprofessional and a waitress just needed to only pitch up in order to get a job because the job was based on good looks alone. In our days many restaurants carry a brand and there is a certain image they would like to portray about themselves and their staff, that is why a good professional waitress resume will go a long way in securing you that perfect waitress job at one of the best paying restaurants in your town.

A well presented waitress resume can make your waitress resume stand out because a lot of waitress resumes are just long lists of previous experiences. Many restaurants are aware that your childhood ambitions were never to be a waitress and that you rather be doing something else than waiting on tables but no restaurant would like to hire a waitress who portrays that negative bored looking vibe even though they understand that they are not number one in your heart.

You can have the most extensive experience in the whole food and drinks industry but if you can't communicate it you will seem under qualified while a novice can seem suitably qualified if her resume is properly structured and includes all the essential resume categories that help decorate her resume with persuasive content. Below is the structure and explanations that will help you write the resume that gets that job.

The Proper Waitress Resume Structure and its contents

Bibliography

Any waitress resume will need to include a part where you introduce yourself and tell them your name, address and contact details. Even though this is a waitress resume some people would like you to include your social security number as they may be interested in doing a background check on you.

Educational History

Talk about what highest grade you achieved and if you were a high flyer include the list of courses you completed and their grades. This is where the difference between a good waitress resume and ordinary one starts.

Employment History

List your employment experiences in your waitress resume in such a way that will accentuate your good qualities. For example if in your previous job one of your functions was to check the customer food before being served. Don't say "Checking food before serving" or the like. You must put it in a way that is more powerful like "Ensuring that food meet the highest standard before serving" or anything close to that.

Key Skills developed

A professional waitress resume is supposed to inform your prospective employers that you are a well rounded and developed person. List good qualities that a waitress is supposed to have and make sure that you make reference to previous experiences.

Self-development

Have you been into a course or some kind of educational seminar, please list those under here as they would make your waitress resume stand out.

References

Just make sure that you inform the person you put as your reference as they might have forgotten you. I can't stress how important this is as it will always ruin a good waitress resume should you put a wrong reference.

"Discover The Hidden Secrets Of Crafting A Professional Waitress Resume That Easily Finds You That Perfect Job!" by visiting my website that will teach you how to make a Perfect Waitress Resume <http://resume-writing-secrets.ecommented.com> I also want to teach you "How to Ace the Interview & Get the Job of Your Dreams - No Matter What Your Experience Level!" by visiting my website that will show you How to ace any job Interview <http://how-to-ace-any-job-interview.ecommented.com>

Resume Writing Blues - They're Just Not That Into You!

You've got a great resume; reads better than a John Grisham novel. Employers would be nuts not to want you. You send out a bunch and wait. You tell yourself any minute they'll be calling. A few days go by and since you know the job market is tough you surmise employers have a lot of resumes to go through and this might take a bit more time than you thought. But when they see your resume the drop ceiling tiles will part and light from the heavens will shine upon them. They'll hear a chorus of "halleluiah" from angels and frantically grab their phones... any time now.

After a week or two you conclude that maybe somehow your esume was lost or your file would not open; maybe your email vent to the spam box. You send another one with a follow up etter. Now another week goes by and you start checking your ontact information. You check the phone number on your re-ume? Finally you ask the BIG question: "What's going on?"

Are you ready for the truth?

The Reasons Employers are: Just Not That Into You

1. No matter how great you are you might not be the right it for an employer. Sometimes employers have ideas of what they re looking for and you are not going to know. Attributes, experi-nce, knowledge, skills, or abilities they have not advertised. Like lating often has hidden criteria, for instance some people appreci-te tall people, others prefer shorter dates. You see in this case: it's hem not you!

2. They're might be somebody better for the position. This ne might be hard to imagine, as great as you are, there could be omeone else better suited for the position.

3. Your resume might not be as great as you are. This is the ne you can do something about:

· You might have used one or more of the 197 words that ou should not use on your resume. Find out about the 197 words ou must avoid and resume writing :http://www.resumedictionary.com/words-that-should-not-be-n-your-resume/> . Check your resume for every word.

· Create your resume to fit the employer. While this takes a it more work, match your knowledge, skill, and ability words with vhat each employer and the industry are using.

· Check your tone: Have several other people (preferably mployers or HR employees) review your resume and cover letter. f your tone is too self centered give up the spotlight: Focus your writing on the needs of the employer and you will find one that loves you!

Just like dating, job hunting is a numbers game. You must job hunt every week to keep the odds in your favor. Keep improving your resume. Make sure what you are sending is relevant to what each employer is looking for and you will find the employer that is "into you" and hears that chorus of "halleluiah" from angels.

Blank Resume Form Free of Charge

Seeking for a job has never been easy and has often times been challenging but every time begins with a resume which in our days even a blank resume form comes at a price. I know that it is a struggle to find a decent blank resume form free of charge that has everything you need in a resume to get that job. I am a firm believer in quality at all times even if you have gotten that blank resume form free of charge it must not be deficient. It must have everything that a good resume would have.

There are a few things you need to know about what is needed in a resume even if its my own free of charge blank resume form.

The Blank Resume Form Free Checklist

1. The design of a resume needs to be eye-catching but must never be over the top as different people have different tastes. You don't want to go over the top for some one that wants a decent look and fill in your resume form.

2. You must fill your resume with relevant information as will be discussed in the proper resume structure theme below. You want your resume to be professional and well remembered.

3. Your resume must be concise and to the point displaying every attribute, skill and experience that makes you clearly stand out among other resumes.

Blank Resume Form Free Proper Resume Structure

? Bibliography

This is where you introduce yourself giving details about your name, address, social security number and the like.

? Educational History

Give a full account of your secondary, tertiary and any other educational background giving both the name of the institution, qualification and year of completion.

? Employment History

Make sure that you list your former employers, the period in which you were in their employment and your responsibilities.

? Key Skills developed

This is where you truly go a step above the rest because you list those qualities which can never be acquired like an education but which can be developed.

? Self-development

Maybe in the course of your employment you have attended a few courses here and there. Ensure that you list all of them in this section.

? References:
Don't lose it here. Put a person you are sure is on your side and clearly remembers you and make sure that you inform them if you are short listed.

Here is your Blank Resume Form Free of Charge

BIBLIOGRAPHY
Name:
Surname:
Physical Address:

Postal Address:

Cell No. :
Work No.:
Home No.:
Email:
Date of Birth:
Social Security No.:
Languages: Understand, Speak, Read, Write;

Secondary Education
Last School Attended:
Highest Grade passed:
Year:
Subject Passed:

Tertiary Education

Institution:
Course:
Status:
Subject Passed
1st Year:

EMPLOYMENT HISTORY

Company name:
Job Title :
Period:
Responsibility:

Key Skills developed:

Self-development:

References:

"Discover The Hidden Secrets Of Crafting A Professional Waitress Resume That Easily Finds You That Perfect Job!" by visiting my website that will teach you how to make a Perfect Waitress Resume <http://resume-writing-secrets.ecommented.com> . I also want to teach you "How to Ace the Interview & Get the Job of Your Dreams - No Matter What Your Experience Level!" by visiting my website that will show you How to ace any job Interview <http://how-to-ace-any-job-interview.ecommented.com> .

Cover Letters - A Few Sample Tips

Cover letter sample are everywhere, different kinds of cover letters where in you will have a lot of ideas in writing your own. And always be aware that if you are applying for a certain job criteria, it is always necessary to include a cover letter. A cover letter sample will help you come up with good thoughts and will also have the idea on how you will sell yourself to the hiring manager. When you write a cover letter, see to it that it will fit to the job description that you are applying. Your skills and competencies should be related to the job that you are applying, remember that having a good cover letter will give you the closer chance of giving the manager the best impression of you.

The truth a behind a cover letter is that it helps the applicant to be distinguished faster, and also, in writing it, you should include your reasons and should explain the interest in the job that is being offered. Be sure that you will review the cover letter sample that you have. Reviewing it will give you a better idea on things that you will write on your cover letter. You can even come up with a better one if you try to do so. And also, upon writing, do not limit yourself in the sample cover letter that you read, instead, make it a way to use it as a reference for your ideas and any other suggestions. Keep in mind that your letter should and must express your interest in a high level and will give you the knowledge in the job that you are interested. This is to give high lights on your experience that is relevant.

Mark Mattey is a writer and entrepreneur. To learn more about cover letter samples <http://www.coverlettersthatkill.com> or cover letter templates <http://www.coverlettersthatkill.com> , visit his website.

How to Write a Resume in English

Writing a resume in English can be different from writing a esume in one's native language. There are many key points to onsider when writing an English resume. The following is a list of elpful tips on writing a resume in English:

An English resume should be created on a word processor. Hand written resumes are not acceptable. Print your resume on igh quality paper.

Do not include a picture of yourself.

Do not put the title Resume or Curriculum Vitae as a heading.

Type your complete name, address, telephone number, fax, nd email at the top of the resume.

The Profile section is where you summarize your skills and xperience. It should be only one or two paragraphs long. Write a esume objective. The resume objective is a brief sentence stating vhat type of work you want to acquire. You should also include our career ambitions.

A resume should be no more than two pages long. Try for ne page. Highlight your positive characteristics by keeping ontent brief and to the point.

Proper grammar and spelling is essential. Use a capital letter at the beginning of a name. Write complete words. That is, do ot use initials for company names or qualifications. Ask an English speaker to check your resume for errors. Use strong verbs uch as: accomplished, encouraged, managed... etc. Use past enses unless explaining your current job and make sure you do ot use "I" in your descriptions.

Spacing: Address: bold and placed in the center of the page

Objective: double space
Experience: double space
Education: double space
Additional Skills: double space

Align everything to the left except your name and address.

When entering your education achievements place your highest qualification first and list the others in reverse-chronological order. Include any degrees or certificates as well as your major. Make sure that you enter the institution and dates you attended. Do not list grades unless they are requested.

Highlighting English Language skills is an extremely important part of the English resume. Under the "Skills" heading, describe your knowledge of the English language. This includes if you are bilingual, fluent in English, and how well you speak the English language.

When entering your career history, place your most recent job first and then list the rest in reverse-chronological order. Include where you worked, dates, name of employer, your position in the company, and your duties.

When listing your skills in an English resume, it is important to highlight technical, professional, and other skills not associated with your career history. Choose skills that are similar (transferable) to the position in which you are applying.

List no more than six achievements from your education, work experience, other experiences (paid and non-paid), and special skills. Highlight unique achievements from your career or education history that will help you stand out from other candidates.

Personal details should be brief and to the point. Details should include your nationality.

Finish your English resume with the statement: References available upon request

The purpose of an English Resume is to sell your qualifications. It is essential to emphasize your education, skills, work experiences, and achievements. A well-written and well-rounded resume can catch the attention of a potential employer.

Learning English <http://www.englishlink.com/> is essential to success when immigrating to a new country. Visit our Resume cover letter <http://www.englishlink.com/testing/JobsIndex_ENG_HTML.asp> section for useful tips.

Cover Letter Templates Work

Even if a lot of people say that cover letters aren't important during the application process, to most HR managers these letters have some significance to their decisions in choosing potential applicants for the roster. The cover letter is basically the first page that the boss will browse through when a resume is submitted, giving him or her an idea of how interested you really are in the job position they are offering. Standards for job applications and employee qualifications have risen up since wages are becoming higher and higher, so usually bosses would narrow down their choices basing on the resumes and documents they receive about the applicant.

Writing an interesting and creative cover letter usually increases your chances of being in that roster of applicants. It serves as your very first impression to the company, so it has to reflect just how interested and how determined you are in getting that job. A lot of applicants would usually learn by downloading a cover letter template and using it as a guide to write their own cover letters. A cover letter template can be very useful since it allow people to pattern it to their own letters basing it one the structure, format, and style. Unfortunately most people would download a generic cover letter template and use that to submit to the HR managers instead, which not only would show them a hint of laziness but the inability to really think out of the box. If you want to avoid such assumptions, then use it as a guide and draft your very own cover letters for every job application process you get into.

Mark Mattey is a writer and entrepreneur. To learn more about great cover letter templates <http://www.coverlettersthatkill.com> or write a great cover letter <http://www.coverlettersthatkill.com> , visit his website.

How Do You Distribute Your Resume

So you think you have produced a quality resume, but you never seem to get any responses to your resume. You then begin to question your own skills and qualifications. The problem may not be with your resume; instead it may be with the way you are trying to distribute your resume. Many people simply fall into the mainstream trap of doing what every other job seeker is doing.

So what may be the real reason why you get no responses to your resume?

Most people use the traditional approach of simply posting their resume on one or two large job boards. The problem with this approach is the competition is extremely high on these larger job boards; which makes it hard for your resume to get discovered.

A better approach for many people would be to distribute their resume on smaller niche job boards where there is less competition. Also, smaller job boards attract more small to medium sized employers. This is because smaller niche job boards are much more affordable for smaller employers to post their job openings. Large job boards charge employers $300-$400 to post one single job opening. This is simply to expensive for many small to medium sized employers; therefore, they use smaller more affordable niche job boards.

There are several companies that specialize in distributing your resume to a large number of smaller niche job boards for a small fee if you want help in this process.

The bottom line is you need to think outside the box of traditional mainstream job seekers. Successful people are always looking for new ways to promote themselves in order to get ahead of the competition.

Chad Surges has a Bachelor's Degree in Business and currently owns and operates the investing website called lucky-dog-investing.com <http://www.lucky-dog-investing.com> . He also invites you to visit his job network website: chiob.com

Resume Writing - Are You a Less Than Perfect Candidate?

Is your resume writing stuck because you have seen the perfect position advertised and had every skill the employer is looking for except one? How do you compensate for a lacking skill when resume writing and still attract the employer?

First, here's a tip from inside HR: Often employers and HR personnel create 'wish list' job qualifications and advertisements. Employers know chances are candidates will not have everything on their list. So do not let the fact that you are not perfect stop you from sending a resume, yet first make an assessment. You do not need to state that you are missing any requirement, though there are some considerations.

Evaluate what you are missing:

1.   Establish if the employer is looking for knowledge or proficiency. Knowledge and proficiency are not the same. Would you rather have a surgeon who has read books on surgery and passed a test, or one who has successfully performed 100 similar surgeries? Education can produce knowledge and proficiency is usually obtained by experience.If the employer is requesting experience, how much experience (proven proficiency) with the specific skill is the employer looking for?

2.   Determine if you can do the job with the knowledge and experience you have.Estimate what percentage of the job will require the absent capability in comparison to the talents you posses. Do you have lattice skills? These are skills that cross over each other and can support the area of the missing one. There might still be some holes (hence the lattice term) or missing knowledge, but you might have enough overlapping knowledge and experience to be proficient.

3.   Investigate how soon you can obtain the missing skill. How much knowledge is required? Is training, additional schooling, or a certification required, helpful or available?

Being the perfect candidate by possessing every skill the employer is seeking is desirable though not always required.

* If a certification or specific training program is required find out how and when you can enroll. If you can do so immediately you can include the fact that you are scheduled to obtain the education what you are lacking.
* If you have enough experience to perform the job without any additional training or education, provide proof with examples of accomplishments on your resume.
* If you have enough expertise to compensate for what is deficient temporarily, be prepared to state in an interview how you can perform with other capabilities until you are trained. Make sure you provide solid examples of accomplishments on your resume for all of your lattice skills. If you are going to convince an employer to give you an interview regardless of a missing item on their list, your other expertise needs to be stated strongly.

When you get an interview for a position your not perfect for, be equally prepared to answer questions about how you will compensate.

Attorney Resume - Blue-Chip Pass For Potential Clients

As we interact with our fellow human beings, we are bound to come in conflict with the law. It is quite understandable because no two persons share the same ideas and opinions on all things. There is going to be a point as well that your actions contradict with what you have long believed and based as a moral ground. Nobody is perfect and there is much more sense of imperfect when people are interacting with each other. Needless to say, if there is a case, it is going to be a field day for lawyers of the nation to turn in their attorney resume.

The jurisprudence of our country sits on two seemingly incongruous and queer rules. One is that a man is treated as innocent until proven otherwise. This is great because everybody is entitled to a day in court before he could be convicted for a day in prison. The second rule, though, is that ignorance of the law excuses no one. So it pays that you know some of its facets. Remember that theoretically nobody is above it and so it does not matter what your social disposition or public status is. When you come in conflict with the law, it is going to be hassling on your part but you got to deal with it. There is no way that you can turn your back on the jurisprudence of the land. The kicker here is that you do not need to know it yourself if you have a lawyer.

There are many legal professionals to choose from for your specific legal needs. Hence, these are some tips on how to find the most capable one for you:

1) Hire a legal hunter. If various industries have job hunters, the field of law has legal hunters. They are specialized professionals who will help you tap the best attorney.

2) Do not underestimate the power of attorney resume. Work-wise, advocates of this profession are pretty much insecure professionals. They know that they are only as good as their last

case. They know that there are lots of competitions around so they tend to put their best foot forward in their resumes.

3) Make further research. Do not just rely on what they say on their resumes. They tend to gloat on their achievements and underscore, if ever they mention at all, on their defeats. It is not so much that lawyers got defeated defending cases sometimes, but be sure to have an idea of the specific circumstance of the cases that they handled previously.

4) Talk to some of the advocates colleagues. The kind of character a certain advocate has is also as important as his batting average. You will not want, of course, an advocate who talks about your case in drinking bars.

The bottom line here is that you must be assured in full confidence of the past performance and character of your advocate. For the lawyers, they should try to go over their attorney resume if it needs some tweaking for the fact that it could be their blue-chip pass to sell themselves to potential clients.

Matthew Stanton writes an article about Attorney Resume and how it can be effective tool to help you find a job in the legal field. Simply visit this site for information at http://www.esqresume.com/

How to Get a Better Job by Blogging (Part Two)

I don't have to tell you how tough the job market is out there. But you now have the tools to break into just about any job you want, just by starting a blog on that subject.

This article is Part Two on the subject of how to leverage the power of blogging to become a recognized authority in whatever field you can become qualified for.

Here is my personal example. About ten years ago, I was a general practice attorney with a small law firm. I really had no specialty at all, but in law school I had taken every estate planning and tax law class that was offered. I really wanted to get a new job with a much better law firm and practice estate planning.

The problem was, my post law school experience was not in estate planning. I spent a lot of my own personal time studying estate law and I kept up on new changes in the law, but I had only written a few wills and one trust. Most of my legal experience was in unrelated areas of law.

Unfortunately, this was ten years ago and I had never heard of blogs and did not have the tech skills to set up a traditional website.

So, looking at this problem from the vantage of, "if I had only known what I know now," here is what I would do now if I were seeking the same job change.

A job seeker today who wants to enter a new field, or wants to move up in an existing field, only needs to start writing a blog on that topic. Post four of five new articles every week and in six months or so this job seeker will become a recognized authority in that field.

Now, add writing online articles on that topic and publishing those articles on various article submission sites or article banks like EzineArticles, GoArticles, ArticleCity or Searchwarp, and the traffic to your blog and your search engine rankings go way up.

Suppose an employer reads one of your articles or visits your blog. Do you think this employer will have any trouble with the fact that you have no actual on the job experience in this field if your knowledge shows through from your articles and your blog? Hardly.

What does it take to succeed with this strategy? You need to have a genuine, real interest in the new field and you must be willing to study this topic on your own to become a real expert in this field. Then you must commit to writing no less than four or five new articles every week on this topic.

Remember what employers are looking for. They want to be assured they are not hiring someone who lacks the qualifications to do the job. But actual on the job experience is not the only way to gain those qualifications. If you are committed to becoming an expert on your own, your blog can show the world what you know.

COPYRIGHT © 2007, Charles Brown

Charles Brown writes about personal branding, search engine optimization, email marketing, social networking and many more ways to market yourself or your business online. Visit him at Web Marketing Coach <http://webmarketingcoach.blogspot.com> and be sure to download one of his free ebooks or subscribe to his newsletter.

Resume Formats - Chronological Or Functional, Which One Best Suits You?

Most resumes will fall into one of these two formatting categories. They both have their advantages for varying situations. So how do you know which one will best highlight your skills?

To simplify the decision process I've written below descriptions of both formats and some basic factors to help you determine which best suits your format....

Chronological Format:

The Chronological format, as it's name indicates is a chronological offering of your work experience. It follows a logical timeline, generally with the most recent job listed first on your resume. It groups together all of your experience and accomplishments associated with each employer.

This format is by far the most commonly used format and it is also the most preferred by employers. They can easily see job progression as well as employment gaps.

Below are some situations in which a chronological resume is best suited.

-You are seeking a position similar to the one you currently hold or one which is in logical succession to your current position.
-You have strong career progression over the past several years and jobs.
-You do not possess recent or large gaps in employment.
-You have worked for well known or reputable employers
-You are applying for a position in a more conservative field.... Ie: engineering, government positions, pilot or accounting.
-You are returning to work after a hiatus (ie: raising children), and returning to the same field/ position.

Being the preferred choice of employers, if the majority of our circumstances match the above indicators, it may be well worth your effort to devise a chronological formatted resume or a variation very similar to the chronological format. However if these situations don't primarily describe your situation, it may be more beneficial to use a Functional Format.

Stay tuned below to the situations which are better suited for a Functional Resume.

Functional Resume

The functional resume is based on skills which are categorized based upon the necessary skills for the job you desire. In a nutshell, you highlight your skills and experience and achievements in one section. Then, generally, an employment section, and is severely "de-emphasized".

Employers often see this format and a "red flag" is raised. The will often start looking for "the problem" and this can then become the focus of the reader. So to use this format is a risk, however, if done well, it can also be a benefit.

Below are some situations where a Functional Resume may be best suited:

-Your strongest experience is not in your most recent or second most recent job.
-You are changing careers
-You are changing fields
-You do not have a strong progression in your work history
-You have a high level of volunteer experience, but not paid experience related to the job you desire
-You are highly over qualified for the job
-You are looking for less responsibility than your current job

Of course, few individuals will fit cleanly into either of these categories. It is always up to your judgment as to which format will be most beneficial for you. These are only guidelines. If you are relatively even in both, it may pay to do a resume in each format and get some feedback from a knowledgeable resume writer or a friend in the Human Resources field.

This is just a start.

This is just the tip of the iceburg. So, to help you get started writing an effective Chronological, Functional or Combination resume that lands interviews, stop by and download your step by step e book, The One Day Resume and also claim your free resume checklist guide at http://www.jobseekersgold.com/One-Day-Resume/Index.htm today!

Here's to your Success!
Dominique

From Dominique Koukol, Author of The One-Day Resume: How to Complete A Quality Resume in a Day and get to the top of the interview list for the job you want.

Resume Style Tips For the Worker Who Can't Get Hired

A resume varies in length between one page to two to three pages. (Anything over three pages is a little bit... pushy!) You know what needs to go in your resume. Information on your educational history, and on your work history. But how you present that history is all important. It's all part of your resume style.

When you give your educational history, for example, you list the school you attended, your major, and specific interests you had. Not a lot of room for originality there. But once you get into the work history, that changes. You have to list all your accomplishments, and you want to present these clearly and coherently.

Then you'll list any certifications you have, or any organizations you belong to. Resume style differs for the type of position you're looking for. Engineers and mechanics will have certifications for example, academics will have lists of organizations they belong to, and so on.

Resume style also refers to the layout of the resume.

A staid style of layout, for example, is to have your name and address as a big, chunky block of text, centered at the top of the page, with the body of your resume below. But resume layout goes in trends and that address can be in one line, all across the top of the page...or even at the very bottom of the page.

However you decide to layout your resume, the key is that the information must be clear and easily accessed. "White space" makes it look attractive.

There's no need to cram all of your details onto a single sheet of paper - these days resumes of two or three pages length are perfectly acceptable.

Keep your resume up-to-date. Even if you are quite happy in your current job, you should always have an eye out for the future. Whenever you accomplish anything of significance, make sure you add it to your resume for future reference.

Looking for a resume tip <http://www.employmentblawg.com/2009/resume-tip> ? Gary Lawson can help! Gary did his fair share of pavement pounding before he realized the key to successful job hunting is in the

RESUME. Today, he writes career-related articles for popular blog EmploymentBlawg.Com <http://www.employmentblawg.com/> . Check out Gary's resumé series when you visit the site today!

How to Write a Good CV

When applying for banking jobs or accountant jobs, your CV is the first time a potential employer will come in contact with you, so you should utilise it as a marketing tool and make a good impression. Before you start writing, you should ask yourself where you are and where you want to go, what experience and qualifications you have, and what your strengths and weaknesses are.

Format

* You should keep your CV under 3 pages
* Put personal details at the beginning
* Work experience should go in reverse chronological order
* Use bullet points to break up the CV
* Print on high quality white A4 paper
* Use examples of managerial and leadership success
* Honestly is the best policy as if you get caught it will make you look bad
* Be as positive as possible about previous work

Content

* Draft out your CV and make sure you get some friends or colleagues to proof read it for you
* Outline instances where you have instigated a particular concept or project
* Talk about how you took this project from start to conclusion
* Detail unique skills that you possess that will make you stand out from the crowd

Your finished CV should be printed on high quality A4 paper, but many employers will ask you to submit your CV by e-mail. When submitting your CV by e-mail you need to remember to use standard fonts and a universal file type like Microsoft word.

Most employers will require you to send a cover letter, but we will save that guide for another post.

Visit my online Travel Blog http://www.onlinetravelblog.co.uk by Tom Sangers.

Biggest Failure of Job Applicants - Not Mentioning Their Accomplishments

In a recent survey, many professional resume writers cited the failure to outline the quantification of job applicant accomplishments as the number one problem with the resumes that they see.

Instead of providing a list of job duties, it is now necessary to show your value to prospective employers by providing specific examples of your top-line achievements. Think in terms of actions and then results of the successful projects that you've completed or been involved with in a team setting.

Look at this way: Employers want to know what your value proposition is as a prospective employee. What is it that makes you stand out over all the other similarly qualified applicants? And more importantly, they use this information to assess what you are going to do for them.

It boils down to three simple things: Employers want to know if you made a company money, saved them money or saved them time. Or, if you are in the non-profit sector, that usually translates into have you increased program services, made more people aware, or broadened your fund raising base?

The key is to always show the value in the work that you've done. You should always keep a list of your accomplishments- a running tab, so to speak. And for those positions that are retroactive, going over previous performance reviews are a good source to find out the top-line achievements that make you stand out from an employer's standpoint.

If you position yourself as someone who is capable of having a significant positive impact on a company's bottom line, you've just made yourself stand head and shoulders over the competition, which will likely get you noticed and into an interview.

Dawn Rasmussen - CTP, CMP
President
Pathfinder Writing and Career Services
PO Box 20536
Portland OR 97294
503-539-3954 phone
503-408-4894 fax
http://pathfindercareers.com/

Advance your career with a professionally-written resume!

Proud member of the National Resume Writers Association

Cover Letter Writing in a Jiffy

Do you need to make a cover letter fast? Well if you are in a hurry to write a cover letter but you are not even sure about one is in the first place, then read on to learn the secrets behind cover letter writing in a jiffy.

If you have absolutely no idea about what a cover letter is, don't fret because writing one need not be a daunting task for you. In fact, cover letter writing is actually a pretty easy skill to master and a definite advantage especially when you are working in a business-like setting. Why is that? Well cover letter writing needs to have a business-like tone, this will help show the interviewer or whoever it is who will be reading your piece know that you are very professional when it comes to handling your job. Aside from showing the interviewer that you have a professional working attitude you should also highlight other key traits about you that you think will serve as an asset to the company.

Do not leave out even the simplest skills that you have may it be being adept in using Microsoft Office or being a licensed driver, you may consider these as just normal things that you can do but believe it or not, employers highly value such things as it as good sign that you will prove to be an efficient employee of the company. If you have other traits or skills that will be a good fit for the company do not to leave those out too.

Mark Mattey is a writer and entrepreneur. To learn more about cover letter writing <http://www.coverlettersthatkill.com> or cover letter format <http://www.coverlettersthatkill.com> , visit his website.

Your Resume - Say No to the Objective Statement

Change can be good. Sometimes there's merit in shaking things up just a bit, especially if you've gotten into a rut.

When you wrote your first professional resume, you may have opened with an objective statement. Many updates later, you're still using the same basic design - and still leading with an objective.

It's time to kiss it goodbye.

Three good reasons to get rid of it:

1) It's too broad

2) It's too narrow

3) It screams out, "Me, me me!"

A broad objective statement is one that's very general and consequently doesn't say anything. It accomplishes only one thing: it takes up up space. Ironically, this is the most valuable real estate on your resume.

(i.e. To secure a challenging position in marketing communications with a dynamic company....)

Potentially just as damaging is the opposite...a narrow objective statement. This one is too specific. One important unintended consequence is that it can exclude you from consideration for other jobs for which you might be well qualified. Because you painted yourself into a box with your opening blurb, your paper gets tossed to the side.

Finally, there's the issue of focus. By its very nature, the objective statement is pretty much all about you. The problem with that? The hiring manager isn't considering your candidacy and your potential fit for the position in terms of what's in it for you. He's not concerned with your objective; he's thinking about his, which is to fill the position.

Leading with a pitch that talks about what you want out of this job, then, is not the most effective method to capture the reader's attention.

Your objective is to get a job. The reader doesn't need a statement to figure that out.

My suggestion? Skip it.

You've got a limited amount of space to work with. Make every line on that resume count.

Rebecca Metschke helps professionals improve their marketability. The author of The Interview Edge (http://www.TheInterviewEdge.com), a comprehensive career guide to career management, she also writes a daily blog posting strategies, tips and advice for those whose careers are in transition.

http://blog.TheInterviewEdge.com

Resume Maker Software - Get a Competitive Advantage Using Resume Maker Software

Using resume maker software is the right option when looking for a job in the market today. You need to make sure your resume stands out from the rest of the pack, as stories of thousands of people applying for the same job become more and more common.

There are several programs out there that offer resume maker software, but many of them, especially the free versions, are not very useful and everyone is using them, so your resume will likely look the same anyway. Remember, you only have one chance to get your resume to the top of the stack, so it is important to find unique ways to make it stand out from the others.

Important Tip: Employers Often Scan Resumes Before Reading the Select Few

Most companies will also tell you that they scan resumes into a computer, looking for certain key words, or even a lack of key words. This is another function where using resume make software can help you. Good software programs will guide you along the way of building your resume that is computer friendly, and loaded with key words that companies are looking for.

Additionally, do not forget the human element to the hiring process. By nature, humans also only scan documents, looking for interesting information. If your resume does not stand out, and immediately make an impact, it will end up in the wrong stack for consideration. Using resume maker software can also make sure your resume makes the right impression.

Using resume make software that will customize your document into one that gets you that personal interview could be the difference between getting a job or not. Of course, any resume is only as good as the person backing it up in the personal interview, but you have to get that interview first to ever have a chance. Don't give up, and keep working hard, good things will come.

For more information on resume maker software <http://www.squidoo.com/resumemaker> , feel free to visit http://www.Perfect-Resume.info. Tips, advice, and top quality resume maker software is reviewed and available there.

Creating a Resume - How Do You Go About It?

In many ways, it is simpler than ever to go about creating a resume. If you purchase a sophisticated word processing application, such as Microsoft Word or WordPerfect, they will include several different templates for resume design.

The most difficult part of creating a resume is deciding what information to put in it! Despite what some people would have you believe, having a college degree certainly opens doors. Not having a degree will prevent you from getting even an entry-level position in most fields.

In order to assure your prospective employer that you have the experience needed for the job, it is as well to participate in as many organizations as possible - relevant to your chosen field - while you're in college. Work experience gained by working on the college newspaper will stand you in good stead when you're applying for a job at a news agency.

Even if you're going to work for an individual who never went to college but, because of their fantastic computer skills, for example, was able to create a multi-million dollar business on their own, chances are that they are going to expect you to have a pretty thorough resume. There's usually room for only one genius in businesses of those kind.

A resume consists of three parts - your education, including the names of the schools you have attended and the specific field of study you followed, your work experience, including names and addresses of companies, and specific work that you performed for each employer. The third part typically features miscellaneous information such as your hobbies, and is where you list your membership in various professional organizations - another important key to make you resume look all the more inviting.

A separate page to your resume is a list of your references. Make sure to talk to your college professors, and your supervisors and associates at all your jobs, so that you can include their names and phone numbers on your reference list.

Desperate for help with resume <http://www.employmentblawg.com/2009/help-with-resume> ? Gary Lawson can help! Gary did his fair share of pavement pounding before he realized the key to successful job hunting is in the RESUME. Today, he writes career-related articles for popular blog EmploymentBlawg.Com <http://www.employmentblawg.com/> . Check out Gary's resumé series when you visit the site today!

Filling in Holes in Your Resume is Really Just a Simple Matter of Gap Management

When it comes to your resume, gap management may be the difference between getting an interview and not being called in at all. Holes in resumes that do not get addressed properly will be filled in with the imagination of those reading your CV and quite often, that which people imagine is far worse than the truth.

If your resume shows extended periods of time wherein you were not a member of the workforce, it is critical that you control how those gaps are addressed. Regardless of whether or not you choose to address these breaks in employment on paper, via the resume itself, or in person, during the interview, you will always want to have a clear and concise explanation for the hole.

An overall strategy for addressing the problem is to keep in mind that the person who is reading your resume is indeed a human being and has, in all likelihood, been in a similar situation at some point in his/her employment history. Some of the reasons for employment gaps could include the following:

*   Relocation
*   Family obligations - the need to care for a loved one
*   Medical - maternity/paternity leave
*   Personal - attending school on a full-time basis for upgrading your skill set
*   Travel

Regardless of the reason, it is best that you be honest. Taking the route of honesty will make you human and communicate your ability to use good judgment and your ability to prioritize needs.

If however, you simply lost your job and just could not get another one for whatever the reason, you may be able to turn this misfortune into a potential benefit for your future employer. By suggesting that it was always your intention to take your time to find the 'right' job or career opportunity rather than 'any' job that will just pay the bills until you find something more suited to your skill set you are again demonstrating the importance you place on the ideal employee/employer relationship.

Remember that every part of your resume should be a positive statement about you. It is never necessary to tarnish your reputation by exaggerating or embellishing your accomplishments. More often, it is just a matter of getting the help of a good wordsmith.

Resumes that do not draw attention to your strengths, experience and education/training serve limited or no purpose. Resumes should focus on your accomplishments. Remember that accomplishments can exist anywhere. Accomplishments and the skills you have learned while doing volunteer work are just as valid as in your paid work experience.

Know that there is no such thing as the 'perfect' resume or the 'perfect' candidate and that you should never be embarrassed by the choices you made. The key to success is to present yourself in a better light than the other candidates who are looking for the same job or career opportunity.

© Salvino 01152009

Mary Salvino MBA is a freelance writer and career/business consultant who lives in Vancouver, BC. She has decades of experience in all aspects of retail management and is a valuable resource to both corporations and individuals in the area of strategic planning.

How to Write a Great Cover Letter

A cover letter is a one-page letter which is sent out with a résumé or CV when you are replying to a job advertisement or when you are contacting a company on spec to enquire about possible unadvertised vacancies.

Every time you send out a résumé or CV it should be accompanied by a cover letter. A letter introduces yourself and your reason for writing, essential when writing cold but not to be overlooked when responding to an ad.

Many people make the mistake of simply rehashing their work history in the letter, but the recruiter has already read your CV and being a busy person, why would he want to read the same information twice? A cover letter should enhance your CV, not repeat it. It is estimated that the majority of employers don't read the cover letter the first time they look at your résumé. If your résumé gets through the first screening, only then will the letter be read. Does this mean it's insignificant? Definitely not! In fact, the opposite is true. At the first reading - scanning would be more appropriate as it's between 10 and 20 seconds - certain CVs will be put in the pile destined for the next round. However, many of them will go no further, except in the direction of the bin. To ensure that your's makes it to the interview pile, you need to write a really good cover letter.

A cover letter should always be addressed to a named person and should be typed (unless you have been specifically asked for a hand-written letter) and set out in the usual business style. It is your opportunity to stand out - to grab the employer's attention and make her want to interview you.

The introduction tells why you are writing. If you are applying for a specific post, you should say where you saw the ad - employers like to track their advertising as this can help them save money in future. Keep it brief, for example "In response to your advertisement, ref 123 in yesterday's Echo, I am writing to apply for xyz." You will then go on to prove, by giving examples, that you have the qualities and abilities to do the job. You can do this by targeting the main keywords in the advertisement and showing clearly that you stand out from the crowd.

You will not need to ask for an interview or to give times at which you are free (unless the advertisement asked for this information) - you will be contacted if you are to be interviewed and will be expected to make yourself available on the interview date.

If you are enquiring about potential vacancies, you'll want to say something which makes the employer sit up and take notice right away. Cold letters are often ignored, binned or filed in the back of the cabinet and forgotten. So something along the lines of "Having recently set up an award winning youth employment program in my home town of X, I was struck by the similarity between your company's mission and my own vision for conquering youth unemployment." By immediately addressing their major concerns and showing that you've already been successful in finding solutions, your letter has a very high chance of being read. The rest of the letter will prove that you have the ability to meet their needs, by giving examples of what you have done and will then ask for the opportunity to meet to discuss the possibility of openings within the organization. You can indicate times at which you are free and you should try to be as flexible as possible.

A well written and highly targeted cover letter could mean the difference between an invitation to attend an interview and no response to your CV. However good your résumé, an excellent cover letter will increase your chances of success.

© Waller Jamison 2007

Need to give your CV and cover letter a makeover? Get step by step instructions <http://www.ukjobapplicationforms.com> and CV templates, plus reports on online applications and transferable skills.

Want to experience more success with your career and personal goals? Download our free goal setting software here: http://www.coolercareers.com/personal-goal-setting.html

Writing Your CV Or Resume - Which Format is Best?

Choosing the right format for your CV or résumé is crucial if you want to present yourself in the best possible light. The best way to set out your CV depends on both your past experience and your next move.

Most of you will be familiar with the traditional chronological CV, which gives your work history in reverse chronological order, starting with your present or most recent job.

Your educational experiences are also listed in the same way.

This CV is a good choice if you have what is sometimes referred to as a "solid track record", usually in the same industry and possibly the same company, often working your way up the career ladder.

If you are considering using a chronological CV, it is essential that you have no obvious or unexplained gaps in your work history, as they will stand out.

Another reason for using this type of CV is to showcase prestigious companies that you have worked for recently. So if your last few employers are likely to impress prospective bosses, you might use this format.

A functional or skills-based résumé focuses on job-related skills and should emphasis those which are most important in the job you are applying for.

This type of CV is useful if you have gaps, are changing career or just starting out in the workplace and have not yet accumulated much work experience. You can focus on transferable skills which you have gained in any area of your life, for example, as a parent, as a student or when doing voluntary work or playing in a team. Just because you haven't got much work experience doesn't nean that you can't do the job and a functional CV will enable you o prove this. So called soft skills, such as communication skills are mongst the most important, with many big employers saying that hey are lacking amongst the workforce. So if you are able to get on vell with people, express yourself competently both orally and in vriting, you have valuable skills, even if you have never worked •efore.

A targeted résumé is similar to the functional type, but ends to focus on more specialized skills and so is likely to be used vhen you are highly skilled in a particular field.

Choosing the right format could mean that your résumé loes not get filed in the bin during the first screening.

Discover how you can sort out your CV :http://www.ukjobapplicationforms.com> to get that Interview.

Want a better career, but need to plan more effectively?)ownload our free goal setting software to help you achieve your areer goals <http://www.coolercareers.com/personal-goal-etting.html> .

Professional Cover Letter Format

There are so many formats needed to write an effective cov-r letter. The format of your paper will generally mean the manner

manner in which the contents and information have been arranged. It can also mean the technical setting and this will particularly refer to the specific requirement of the position or course you are applying for and the manner in which it will be submitted. Keep in mind that the format could mean any of the above or could include all of the above features.

In most cases, your prospective employer or the course you are apply to may ask you to compose upon the requirements of the company. Make sure that you follow all the requirements of that format. But if there is no specific format of the cover letter, you can include the following points:

Your cover letter should contain your contact information. This should be at the opening of the document you write. Keep in mind that you are applying either for admission or for employment. It is normal that the results will not be given to you instantly. This is the more reason why your contact information must be included in your cover letter for resume. This should include your postal address; your telephone number and your email address. Remember to include your mobile number, your office number and your home number.

Continue with the date. The format for the date will also vary. But it is common to start with the month, day and year. Next is the title, the name and address of the organization.

The first paragraph of the cover letter should contain your objective of submitting it or the curriculum vitae. Remember to include how you got information about the organization or job opening. There should also be some essential information about you in person.

Your second paragraph should give information on why you are very concerned about the job opening, the organization or the program of study. Remember that to make mere declarations of your interest in the position or program is not enough. Mere declarations will lead you to nowhere. This means that you must research about the organization or the program of study to be able to prove that you have sufficient interest.

The format of the document should also take account of an inclusion of a fact that you would want to be given a chance to prove your worth through an interview. Make sure you have personally signed your cover letter. In almost all cases, you will be required to type your document. You can get considerable cover letter help in writing this cover letter by looking at cover letter samples or cover letter examples available over the internet.

Dilan Davis is a certified cover letter <http://grandresume.com> writer at GrandResume.com who provides useful information about cover letter format <http://grandresume.com/blog/resume-writing/grandresume.com-your-source-of-professional-resumes/176> .

Free Resume Template

A template is usually used to generate the required information which will be used to formulate the final resume and customize he same to meet the requirements of a job opening. For a good education resume or an academic resume the main information is the job profile. If the profile of the advertised job matches your qualification and experience then it is safe to apply for the same. But in most cases this is where most applicants fail.

When you consider how to write a resume or CV the initial information that needs to be included in the template is the contact. It will contain your name along with your full contact address. It is important that you provide only the correspondence address. This way the potential employer will have less difficulty in contacting you. Also provide your contact numbers and email address. Now many employers forward the offer letter to your email address, hence ensure that you provide the correct information. Objective is one factor which can be included in the template. In most cases this gives the professional objective of the applicant in accordance to the job profile. But if you really want to keep this portion, keep it short within a sentence or two. In some cases a well written objective works wonders for the applicant.

For an experienced person the career highlights are the most important area. This part of the template deals with the key skills, achievements and experience in a bullet format. Highlight the points which are relevant to the applied position. This will give the potential employer and idea that you are enthusiastic about the job and has taken great care in constructing the resume for the same. In some cases you can disregard the qualification aspect in the template, because you will anyway include the same in a chronological format final resume. However, if the position demands any specific qualification you need to include the same in the template. When writing down the details of your experience, site the information in a descending manner. First include the details of your current position along with the duration of the employment and the place of work. Give information of your job responsibilities and the achievements you have attained during the tenure. In this way include all the experiences in an orderly fashion.

Last but not the least he free resume template should include the details of your education in a descending format. Give some information about your interests and skills and sum up the resume template with the references. This is usually required when you are through with the interview and is about to receive the offer letter. But in some cases this is required at the very beginning. Use the templates to compose a good resume for your career ahead.

Dilan Davis is a certified professional resume <http://grandresume.com> writer at GradResume.com who provides useful information about free resume template <http://grandresume.com/blog/tag/free-resume-template>

What a Cover Letter Can Do That a Resume Can't Do

Most people assume a cover letter is just an introduction. And that your resume is what an employer will focus on. Things can hardly be further from the truth. This "introduction letter" is more important than your resume. A cover letter is what opens the eyes of the employer, grabs their attention and encourages them to read your resume. In other words, that so called opening letter is what "sells' you to the employer.

Your cover letter should be well written and point out the facts as to why you're the best candidate for the job. The letter is like a little salesman telling the employer all your benefits and why you're the best person for the job. Your resume in reality is just the facts about your pass experience and what your have done.

Think about your letter this way. It connects all the dots (the facts on your resume) together and paints a picture for the employer. That picture is what "sells" you to the employer. This picture is what makes the employer want to read your brilliantly crafted resume.

Remember, in today's economy, the employer most likely has received any where from 25 to 225 resumes for the job you're applying for. This is not the time to have the typical attitude that most job seekers maintain, which is: "employer; you have a job, I have a resume, and I hope to hear from you soon".

In today's tough job market, it's the person who stands out above the crowd that has the best chance of getting the job. The person that can "sell' himself or herself to the employer is the one rewarded with a job interview.

So take time in writing that all important Cover Letter, as it can do more for you than any well written resume could ever accomplish.

For more information on how to write a killer Cover Letter that gets job interviews, visit us at http://jobhuntingresources.info as well as other good tips for finding that next job

Resume Assistance For You

Writing a "killer" resume is not rocket science. You write down your educational qualifications, and you write down the various jobs at which you've worked, and your duties in each position. What you do not want to do is lie on your resume. People have done that in the past - high-profile people - they always get found out and lose their job in consequence. (Of course, if you're ome kind of sports coach, another job will come along thanks to he old boy network, but you can't count on that in the real word!)

However, many people who are perfectly find at their cho-en profession have a difficult time creating their own resumes. Vell, you can find resume assistance as easy as performing a earch on the internet. There are plenty of qualified wordsmiths ,ho can help you craft your resume so that its is "just right."

Resume assistance comes in a variety of ways. You can heck out books from the library that will give you advice on verything from writing your resume to how to act in an interview. 'ou can hire a business coach to help you out. Or you can check ,ut the many online services.

The economy is lousy. More and more people, across the pectrum from blue collar to white collar jobs, will be sending out heir resumes desperate for work. It behooves you to have the nost professional resume possible, and if it's been a long time ince you've had to apply for work, it might also make sense for ou to talk with a business coach who can give you mock inter-iews to help you prepare for the real thing.

In addition to sending your resume to potential employers, ou should also post your resume online at your own private vebsite. It should be a PDF, so that your potential employers can ,ok at it, but not acquire your email address or phone number.

Looking for a resume format sample :http://www.employmentblawg.com/2009/resume-format-ample> ? Gary Lawson can help! Gary did his fair share of pave-nent pounding before he realized the key to successful job hunting s in the RESUME. Today, he writes career-related articles for ,opular blog EmploymentBlawg.Com :http://www.employmentblawg.com/> . Check out Gary's resumé eries when you visit the site today!

Resume Tips For Financial Candidates

In today's business environment, many candidates in the financial services arena, including banking, mortgage, and investment management, are hedging their bets and considering their options in the job market. However, they are concerned that little, if anything, will be available within their own field, so they plan to try their luck in other arenas. So what can you do with your resume if you find yourself in a similar situation?

Don't Hide and Don't Explain Away

One of the most common mistakes made by candidates who find themselves unemployed as a result of a bankruptcy, an acquisition, or a major downsizing, as well as candidates who are still employed but by a company or industry that is much maligned, is to attempt to hide information. Many others will spend a significant amount of space on their resume trying to explain how the predicament the company found themselves in was not their fault.

Employers don't want to read that type of information because they are not interested in the type of candidates for whom nothing is ever their fault. Don't get me wrong. The fact that your company went belly up or that stockholders demanded a massive layoff to achieve a temporary boost in the stock price is most certainly not your doing. However, employers get the impression from candidates that state that information on their resume that they are the type of person who typically blames things on everyone else. With the number of financial services organizations struggling, going under, or taking massive amounts of government-really taxpayer-money, a lot of job seekers will need to have a strategy on how to address these situations. Most will sympahize and some will empathize with your experience, as long as you don't come across as desperate. So be straightforward about the companies you have worked for without listing all the reasons why you are no longer them.

Focus Your Resume

Do your best to target your resume for specific types of positions. You may feel like your experience does not translate easily into other areas, but that is simply not true. The more focused you get, the easier it will be to identify what employers are looking for and to gear the content of your resume to match their needs. Regardless of industry, employers today are looking for people that have a track record leading teams, improving processes, increasing revenue, and driving cost savings.

Don't Lose Hope

I know it is easier said than done, but don't lose hope. There is tremendous value in what you have done and even in the companies you have done these things for. Be confident in your background and don't be squeamish about listing all of the information on your resume.

So who am I anyway? Why do I think my advice is so valuable?

My name is Stephen Van Vreede. My company is called No Stone Unturned, and I have spent 15 years on both sides of the corporate hiring experience.

The short story is that I have an MBA in Marketing from Villanova University and a dual B.S. degree in Finance & Logistics from the University of Maryland. I am a certified professional résumé writer (CPRW) and a member of the Professional Association of Résumé Writers and Career Coaches (PARW/CC). As I mentioned, I paid my dues in the corporate world eventually running a large-scale call center for a major truck rental company, and I have spent the past 7 years with No Stone Unturned, assisting job seekers in achieving their goals.

In February 2009, I launched a new group job hunting networking site: NoddlePlace.com. It is absolutely FREE to join, and you have access to everything on the site. Come check it out at NoddlePlace <http://www.noddleplace.com> . You can also follow me on Twitter <http://www.twitter.com/noddleplace> .

Need Help With Resume?

If you need help with resume construction, there are plenty of places you can turn to. As far as the overall "look" of your resume, you can find a variety of examples in your word-processing software package. The look of your resume is mostly up to your choice...whatever you think looks most professional...or most appealing to the people in the field you're trying to enter.

The look is cosmetic and it all comes down to personal choice. Do you want your address and phone number each on a separate line, centered in the middle of the page, or aligned left? Or do you want to save room by having all that address information in one line running across the top of the tape, which will leave you that much more room for the important things - your education and work history.

Typically, the years during which you attended school, or the years during which you worked at a particular job, are aligned left, and to the right of these dates, indented, is the name of the school/employer, your position, and your duties. You'll be able to distinguish these different layouts when you look at sample resumes.

The look of the resume is almost as important as the information it contains. It presents an aspect of your personality. If it doesn't look professional, then you don't look professional.

Don't be ashamed to ask for help with resume construction from professional people whose business it is to assure you that you are presenting your best foot forward. More than just overseeing the "look" of the resume, they'll make sure that all the information contained in the resume - your schools -- majors, minors and general courses, are properly called out. They'll also make sure that your work experience stands out as it should.

The resume is your foot in the door to a new career. Make sure it's a foot with wingtips, not a tennis shoe!

In need of resume assistance <http://www.employmentblawg.com/2009/resume-assistance> ? Gary Lawson can help! Gary did his fair share of pavement pounding before he realized the key to successful job hunting is in the RESUME. Today, he writes career-related articles for popular blog EmploymentBlawg.Com <http://www.employmentblawg.com/> . Check out Gary's resumé series when you visit the site today!

Cover Letter Are Not Cover Letters - They Are Sales Letters

When constructing your Cover Letter, you must think of it as a "Sales Letter". It's the instrument that will open more doors for you than your resume. Resumes do not sell. They are not written to sell. And in most cases, unless your resume is outstanding, it can actually end up hurting your chance of landing the job.

Therefore, your Cover Letter is the only chance you have to sell yourself to the hiring manager, for the chance of getting an interview. This is where you have an opportunity to out shine your competition. A carefully written letter with the right marketing terms can open the door for you over your competition. Remember in today's world you are most likely going up against 25 to 100 people for the same job opening.

The vast majority of job seekers simply throw's something together to attach to what they hope is an outstanding resume. Today's hiring mangers want to be impressed with a job applicant. They want an individual who not only meets all the requirements of the job, but will also be an asset to the company. Put yourself in their shoes. Everyday they see the same old boring cover letter attached to an average quality resume. You need to stand out from the crowd.

By having a carefully crafted Cover Letter that speaks to the hiring manager and grabs their attention, you can be assured of getting an interview. A brilliantly worded cover letter is the greatest edge you can have over your competition and most job seekers fail to understand this fact.

Elements you should have in your cover letter are how your skills and background can make a substantial positive difference for the company. Write about your strengths as to how they can be directly applied for the company's benefits. Use the best features

rom your resume to hammer home any points you want to high
ight and write about them.

Remember, your Cover letter should be hyper focused on
etting you the interview and Hired. That's all the "Sales Letter" is
upposed to do. Sell you to the hiring manager.

for more information on how to write a killer cover letter,
risit us at http://jobhuntingresources.info as well as learning
bout other tips for finding that next job

Top 7 Resume Writing Tips

When writing a resume it is important to remember these
pieces of paper represent who you are. The person whose job it is
o judge whether their company should invest time and money to
lire you has to pull you from other candidates based on what you
vrite. It is very important not only to you being employed but can
lso factor huge into the type of wages offered from the company.
This is why I have included a list of important items when writing
l resume.

1. Be Specific and show purpose in writing your resume

Know your target, cater it to them and make sure it is on
point.

2. Back up strength

When you state a quality you possess (i.e. disciplined, problem solver) connect it to something work related.

3. Use Bullet Points

Bullet points draw attention and give specifics

4. Clean and Crisp

Make sure the overall look of resume is pleasing to the eyes

5. Be current with information

Do not put work experience mowing yards when you were 17 unless it is relevant to the job.

6. List important information first make sure you get there attention when they read it

7. Consider getting professional help

This may be the most important help. It is so vital to landing the job of your dreams it may be a good idea to get it out of the hands of amateurs. Just like the use of Lawyers, Mechanics, and Accountants sometimes it is necessary to get professional help. This could be the single most important aspect in landing a quality job. Also this will be a small we compared to what you will make with the salary they will being willing to compensate you with.

Visit Resume Wizard <http://www.needajobblog.com> for more tips to land the job and salary of your dreams

Crafting the Perfect CV - Perils, Pitfalls and Pratfalls

School-Boy Errors

Including your Date of Birth: You're advised not to include your date of birth for discrimination purposes. Besides, if you do you run the, admittedly slight, risk of getting it wrong. You'll soon find that a few misplaced digits can cause a great deal of trouble. Very few firms will offer executive jobs to people younger than 14 or older than 140.

Using the wrong contact details: Perhaps the cruelest of mistakes. Re-check those digits or you'll be the only girl not at the dance.

Submitting an unprofessional Email address: Popping up in the inbox as 'hotmale@hotmail.com' or 'Suburbancowboy69@yahoo.com' will not result in your appointment as Travel Director. Jobs in the upper echelons just don't work like that.

Peppering your work with Misspellings: If you can't be trusted with a spellchecker you can't be trusted with a company. Don't even consider applying for executive travel jobs by claiming you used to work in 'Tennereefay'.

Redeemable Transgressions

Leaving Unexplained Gaps - Don't try and hide those 2 years you spent as a roadie for Metallica. Who knows what horrors they might imagine instead?

Breaking the two-page rule - The secret of 'image' is judicious editing. Let your C.V. present only the cream of your achievements and save a little something for date night.

Using empty clichés - Put yourself in the employer's position. Sooner or later phrases such as, 'Good communicator' and

'Works well in a team' begin to blur into obscurity. You might as well write 'Regularly digests solids' or 'Breathes 78% Nitrogen' for all the good it will do you. If you're aiming for executive jobs, show proof of your excellence, not a repertoire of empty claims.

Indefensible Indictments

Lying - If you once drove three of your mates to Dieppe on a 'Booze Cruise' then don't claim you spent 5 years as an International Travel Director. Jobs at that level often aren't as easy as them seem and one would like to think you'd be caught out.

Using friends as a reference - Unless your friend is a talented web-designer and a vocal impersonator on a level with the 'Fonejacker' you will not pull this off. In fact, like many Con Artists, you may end up putting more effort into the deception than it would take to make the same profit from legal pursuits.

The rest, of course, is up to the quality of your presentation. With competent, clear and direct writing there is no reason that you shouldn't secure the interview for the job that you deserve. If possible try and read as many of other people's C.V.s as you can and try and work out exactly what the employer is looking for. If you know that, and are confident you've the relevant experience, the most desirable executive jobs should be well within your grasp.

Gail Kenny is the managing director of Gail Kenny Executive Search, a recruitment agency specialising in executive travel jobs <http://www.gailkenny.com> . The site caters exclusively to talented individuals with skills and experience to succeed in the travel management, and businesses looking for such candidates.

How to Write Cover Letters - 7 Golden Tips to Learn How to Write Cover Letters

How to write cover letters? So many people wonder how to write cover letters effectively. This is not hard. You just need to follow a few guidelines and you will be on your way. Let's have a quick look at 7 golden rules.

Writing a good cover letter is the key to attract potential employers. Yet many people seem to stumble upon a few simple rules to craft a well-presented and effective cover letter.

*Golden rule #1

Use normal paper when you write your letter. You want to stand out with the quality of your writing skills not the quality of your paper, its colour or the fancy font you have used.

*Golden rule #2

Do a little bit of research and address the person you are writing the letter to. DO NOT use pre-made structures such as "To Whom it may concern" as it is too impersonal.

*Golden rule #3

Do some research about the company you want to join. If you mass-write letters, you MUST adapt each letter to the particular characteristics of each position. There is nothing more annoying for an employer than reading a written piece with the name of another company in it.

*Golden rule #4

When you talk about yourself, be straightforward. There is no need for you to tell a long story about your life in the cover letter. If you do, it might end up in the bin.

*Golden rule #5

Show off. You need to show off your qualities in your letter and what you can bring to the company. Ask yourself why the recruiter would hire you instead of someone else. You are better than the other applicants because you are able to bring the notion of efficiency, dedication and commitment to another level. You are unique. Keep that in mind. There is no need to eat humble pie when you are writing a cover letter. It is your time to shine. Of course, do not go too far. When the job interview comes, you will need to back up your claims.

*Golden rule #6

This is an aspect which is, interestingly enough, often underused by applicants; your letter does not need to be breathtakingly original yet you should display a bit of personality in it. What I mean by personality is, of course, humour. If you make your recruiter smile when reading your letter, you win. Needless to say that it'd better be a smile than a smirk. In other words, make him smile because you are displaying a witty sense of humour. Not because he is laughing at your spelling inaccuracies.

*Golden rule #7

This brings me to my last point: Spelling. It does not matter whether you are John Grisham or the guy next door. Your cover letter has to be mistake-free. Ask a friend to proofread it for you.

There is a secret sentence used in one out of a thousand cover letters. Use this secret sentence and you will dramatically increase your chances of getting a job interview. Visit us if you want more tips on how to write cover letters <http://www.squidoo.com/Effective-Cover-Letter> . Take action now!

Administrative Cover Letters

Tips To Compose Administrative Cover Letters

While carrying out any preliminary exploration, you must be aware of the fact that your responsibility will include a coordination and performance of certain staff responsibilities as well as be a connection to other units within the organization. You will also have to provide some form of administrative assistance to the organization. Remember that this may equally mean you have to take giant steps at solving problems within the organization. Your ability to carry out all these duties will be manifested in your cover letter.

Make your cover letter stand out above those of others. This means only those qualities which should be considered best or outstanding should be included in the cover letter and these should be well related to the job in question. Remember that this is what is going to be used to make your application considered ahead of other applicants.

Make sure your cover latter is addressed to the appropriate person. There are lots of applicants who fail to mention the right person to whom the cover letter should go to. Always steer clear of generalities like using the phrase "To Whom It May Concern". Prove to the employer that you know what you are doing and are aware of the implications of what you are doing. If a particular name of the person to whom the cover letter should be addressed to is not provided in the job advert, it is your duty to call and find out the name and title of the person.

Keep everything short and simple. Your cover letter should always be composed in not more than a page. Remember that cover letters of two and more pages will be taken to mean that you can be a complex or complicated person to work with. Make sure that your language is simple and to the point. Avoid effusive language or wordy phrases that may end up making your cover letter complex. Keep in mind that the employer has more cover letters or applications to go through and may simply shove your cover aside for lack of clarity or simplicity.

Administrative cover letters should be attention grabbing and should aim to sell the applicant. This means you should honestly state only what you can do and explain how you can import what you have into the organization. Remember that every employer needs positive results. Have someone reliable to read through your cover letter to make sure that it sounds convincing. You can get considerable cover letter help in writing this cover letter by looking at cover letter samples or cover letter examples available over the internet.

Dilan Davis is a certified resume <http://grandresume.com> writer at GrandResume.com who provides useful information about administrative cover letters <http://grandresume.com/blog/cover-letter-writing/administrative-cover-letters/85> .

Resume Writing Tips - 4 Vital Things to Remember When Writing a Resume

In this article, I'm going to reveal some resume writing tips to help you gain an advantage over other applicants.

In such a competitive world, you need to prepare as much as you can. After all, it's difficult to land an interview without an impressive resume that catches the employer's eyes. Here's some vital resume writing tips to remember:

1) Physical Demands.

You need to make sure that your resume is printed on nice quality paper. Make sure it's clean. No smudges. No crinkles.

This advice might sound superficial to you but the employer will consider how your resume looks like. It's an extension of yourself. If your resume is dirty and disorganized, what would that say about you?

2) Keep Everything In Order.

This is one of the resume writing tips you should pay close attention to. Arrange your accomplishments and work experiences in proper categories. Don't mix them all together. Always start with your most recent, because it helps your employer get a better understanding of who you are now.

Personal information is usually placed at the end of the resume. While you must keep it short, don't just put your birth date or place there. Include relevant hobbies, interests, and skills that might be useful for the position you're applying and help you gain an advantage. For instance, listing down traveling as an interest will give the impression that you're outgoing and adventurous.

3) Never Fabricate.

Never, ever put something untrue in your resume. This is one of the most vital resume writing tips. Don't exaggerate on your skills either. If you can barely speak Italian, don't put down that you speak it fluently. Even if something like that impresses the employer, it's bound to get you into trouble sooner or later.

4) Double Check For Typos Or Grammatical Errors.

A resume with even just one typo is a turn off. This gives them the idea that you didn't even review your work properly. While something like this should be common sense, and should not even be part of resume writing tips, you'd be surprised at how many still make this mistake.

These resume writing tips are very important. They help create an idea of the kind of person you are, even before the interview.

Want to get your dream job? Get FREE tips and video on how to write a cover letter <http://www.squidoo.com/how-to-write-a-cover-letter-for-a-resume> that grabs attention like a magnet. Know the secrets of preparing for a job interview <http://www.20daypersuasion.com/job-interview.htm> that gets you hired on the spot.

How Do You Know the Cover Letter is Good Or Not?

Such a cover letter should be an effective written work. It does not always have to be specific to or look alike with what you have in most common types of cover letters. In fact the danger is that if there are so many similarities, the job seeker may be tempted to copy this to meet the specific needs of his or her cover letter. The truth about this is that sooner or later, this will be discovered because in will be shown on your job performance. This is the more reason why you must always have some form of creativity if you have to succeed while working in an organization. These are simply meant for creating an appropriate picture of the document in your mind. The contents may be something that you have never stumbled upon or had the chance to read. Thus you can make your own cover letter alive by learning from good examples written by real professionals.

There are so many sources to look at such good examples of professional writing. You may need to search for help from more experienced people to get the job of your choice. If you are applying for a position that you think you are virtually blank about everything from the start, you can always make recourse to example cover letters. But remember that you must personally know what you want ahead of resorting to some other form of help.

When you look at perfectly written samples, there are certain things which must prick your mind. Is the composition of the cover letter relevant to what you are required to do? Go back and read the job description very well. If you are not making an application to a specific position, make sure that you have researched and understood the goals or objectives of the organization. Are these examples of cover letters the best you can think of? With this in mind, think of the internet as well as your school library. These kind of paper are available everywhere. But it is not on any examples that you can lean on. The best advice is to rely on sources from the library rather than the internet. When an example is found in the library, there is guarantee that it has been tested and proven to meet academic excellence.

Examples of good cover letters should always be specific and should be tailored to meet the requirements of every type of the document. These sample-works are meant for you to glance through and get some inspiration in personally writing your own cover letters. Look at the format of the paper and make sure that everything meets the requirements of its writing.

Dilan Davis is a certified cover letter <http://grandresume.com> writer at GrandResume.com who provides useful information about examples of good cover letters <http://grandresume.com/blog/cover-letter-writing/finding-examples-of-good-cover-letters/115> .

Help With a Cover Letter For a Resume

You may never know this, but the difference between a person seeking for a job and a person professionally qualified for that job can only be found in an effective cover letter that accompanies the resume. To compose this, you must know that this is one of the most serious forms of writing. In fact, this should be seriously taken as writing the class exam. Remember that your efforts will be worthless if you eventually fail to find a job.

When a cover letter has to accompany a resume, there are so many things that will be inferred from it by your prospective employer. When this is properly written and well presented in the proper and correct format, it will first of all be taken as an effective and professional way to let your prospective employer know about your capabilities. However, remember that stating your capabilities in your cover letter should not restate what is found in the resume. The main aim of this is to let your future employer be aware of what you can do and how this can be related to what is found in your resume. You will also have to carry out some in-depth study about the requirements or needs of the organization or the position that you are applying for. This will let the employer now that you can very well relate and work as per the needs of the organization. It will also communicate to the future employer that you are the most likely candidate that should fill that position.

This may not be your first time of writing a cover letter that will be used as an "entrance door" of the main application document. The mistake that most job seekers do is that they write one cover letter and attach it to or they simply copy cover letter examples and attach it to every resume they submit. You should never assume that the goals or needs of every organization are the same. Even if they are the same, the requirements of the position you are applying for may not be the same. Every cover letter should be specifically written to meet the requirements of each resume you write.

Make sure you use a standard format for writing the document. Remember that organization at this stage will be used to prove how organized you may be if you are eventually employed. If you are composing more than one cover letter, make sure you address each to the appropriate person. Otherwise it will be a horrible mistake on your side.

A Cover letter for a resume should be concluded with what you think you can offer that is lacking in the organization. Keep in mind that every employer will want to see what innovations you can bring into the organization. Remember to demonstrate how you are going to implement this. This is also applicable when you are not applying for any specific position. You can also get significant cover letter help in writing this cover letter by looking at cover letter samples available over the internet.

Dilan Davis is a certified cover letter <http://grandresume.com> writer at GrandResume.com who provides useful information about cover letter for resume <http://grandresume.com/blog/cover-letter-writing/cover-letter-for-resume/132>

Resume Advice - Optimizing Your Resume For Federal Government Jobs

Long ago, employers posted job openings in the newspaper, and were then flooded with a stack of paper resumes from interested applicants. At smaller companies, the task of weeding through the resume pile was often delegated to low-level workers who told to scan for specific criteria and sort the pile into one large stack of "No" and a small stack of "Maybe." The maybe stack would then be passed up to the HR department for further study.

Now, that same flood of resumes is filtered electronically and much of that first-level scanning is done by a computer program. Recruiters can simply search on specific keywords and only pull up resumes that include those specific words. So how do you get past the computer program and get your resume in front of a recruiter for government jobs? And how do you make sure that recruiter sees exactly what he's looking for?

YOU GOTTA HAVE GOALS

First, you have to know what job you're looking for. Sometimes recent college graduates, or people who have been laid off, become so wrapped around the necessity of finding a job that they forget to think about which job. They submit the same resume to a dozen different postings without tailoring anything. This approach is sort of like asking out every girl at a bar at the same time: no one is very impressed.

Look through the job postings on USAJobs.gov. If you are certain you want to perform a certain job function, or if you know you want to work for a certain agency, carefully read several postings for open positions that meet your criteria. Understand the keywords used in the posting - everything the hiring manager wants to see is all right there. If you fit the jobs, print out the postings. Write on them. Mark them up. Highlight the parts that sound like you.

KEYWORD OPTIMIZATION IN YOUR RESUME

Use the job postings you printed and marked up to create an outline for your resume. Organize it based on the skills and requirements that are the most important to the hiring organization. For example, if the posting states several times that you must have excellent writing skills, put writing skills at the top of your outline. Use the exact same words in your outline that were used in the posting so that you hit the right keywords.

Then, spell out the specifics of how you have met all the requirements. Be specific, use numbers to quantify your accomplishments, but don't get too wordy.

BREVITY IS THE SOUL OF WIT

Keep it short and simple. Remember, your resume may be one of hundreds. If it is multiple pages in length, the recruiter will likely get bored before he reaches the end. You don't have to share your whole biography here, only the details that are relevant to this particular position. Remember who will be reading it and how - in a hurry, with a specific objective. So keep your writing focused on the requirements of the posting.

GET A SECOND OPINION

Always have a friend, relative or associate read over your resume before you post it. Back in the old days, when resumes had to be printed, we probably caught more of our own typos and misstatements. In the digital age, it is just so easy to throw something together and send it off into the system without a second glance. The recruiter at the other end, however, will definitely be turned off by glaring errors.

Spell-check is a good start, but it can't check for misused words and the grammar check is not infallible. Be sure to read your resume aloud to yourself to catch errors. Then find another actual human - preferably one with an eye for English - to read though the document for you. Provide them with a copy of the job posting so that they can cross-check against the job requirements. If you have a coworker help you with this, they will probably point out other skills relevant to the posting that you haven't mentioned.

SUBMIT YOUR RESUME

Only after setting your goals, outlining, editing, and getting a second opinion should you submit your resume. Yes, this process will take more time than broadcast-style job applications, but the result will be a highly-specific resume that is tailored directly to the job you want. The federal government hiring managers will be able to see that your skills match their needs, and you will have a much better chance of success.

There's more competition than ever for choice federal government jobs <http://www.jobmonkey.com/governmentjobs/> so you must make sure that your resume is perfectly tailored. Lisa Jenkins, a career writer for the free JobMonkey website, shares her knowledge about job search strategies online. Find out how to find work with the government, including border protection jobs <http://www.jobmonkey.com/governmentjobs/customs-border-protection.html> and airport security screening employment with federal agencies such as the Transportation Security Administration and Customs and Border Protection.

Let Your Resume Stand Out

In this job market, it pays to stand out. While you will always need a printed, great looking resume to take to potential job interviews, the use of technology can greatly boost your chances at that dream job.

With the use of the internet, a growing number of people are turning to online resumes. How better to make yourself stand out than having a link to information all about you on a personalized web page? The tools available to make this possible are plentiful.

Just like a paper resume, your web based one should make a statement about not only your abilities, but your personality as well. While it is important to be unique, being professional is of greater importance. Your resume should reflect your capabilities and your strong points. This is far more important than having a flashy website.

Also, it is important to keep your resume in some sort of order just like a printed one. Keeping it orderly instead of scattered will show off more professionalism. Keep your contents in order too - an order that people who read it are familiar with. For example, keep your work experience listed in reverse order with your most recent job first. Under each, have the time frame in which you worked there and a brief job description of your responsibilities.

It is important to keep your education background on this type of resume as well. Any higher education you have accomplished should be listed. It is wise to refrain from adding too much personal information. You need to save something for the interview. While you want to peak the interest of a potential employer, it is wise to keep most of your personal background to a minimum.

More or less, the ideas presented and the layout for your resume both in paper form or online should remain the same. The same information is needed on both, but showcasing yourself with an online resume is beginning to be just as important as the job interview itself.

For resume examples <http://www.visualcv.com/www/examples/> , visit VisualCV. A better cv resume <https://www.visualcv.com/cv_resources/cv_templates> online can help you stand out from the crowd. Heidi Ball is a freelance writer.

Creating Your First Resume

It can be a scary thing putting on to paper all that you know or all that you've done. When applying for a new job however, it is critical to have a decent tell all resume. Worrying about writing your resume is fairly common. Just remember that the main goal is to generate interest in you and what you can accomplish, in turn getting those interviews!

Here are a few pointers for the time you begin writing your resume.

Keep it detailed, yet simple. You want to pique interest in yourself and your abilities, but you do not need to tell a history of your life. Simply ask yourself before you put something down the following: "Is this information pertinent to the jobs I'm applying or? Will it show I can add value to their company?" If not, it's best not to include it.

Communicate your strengths clearly. If you do this, potential employers will want to meet you.

Research what jobs are available and apply to those that interest you. Look for jobs that have the skills you possess and apply to those. Be sure that your resume reflects those skills.

It never hurts to read other resumes from friends or online, giving you a starting point. You want it simple, full of information about your skills and clean in appearance. Many are turning to online resumes verses the old paper version, having websites unique to them that tell everything a future employee would want to know.

Don't worry about not having enough experience to create a great resume. Once you really start thinking about it, you'll find from past experiences you have plenty to expound upon. Be sure to include your personality characteristics that would be beneficial to the job. Your computer skills and knowledge is a must for your resume. Also education and your accomplishments from school plus any awards you might have received. If you have any sort of work history, be sure to include it. Finally, put your best references forward!

It's easy to create a great resume using many different tools and even websites that are now available.

For great ideas for creating a resume <http://www.visualcv.com/quickstart/> , visit VisualCV http://www.visualcv.com/quickstart/), a new way to create internet based resumes. Heidi Ball is a freelance writer.

INDEX*

205

206

208

220